OF HEALING AND FINDING HOME

JEFF GAURA

Trilogy Christian Publishers
A Wholly Owned Subsidiary of Trinity Broadcasting Network
2442 Michelle Drive
Tustin, CA 92780

Copyright © 2021 by Jeff Gaura

Scripture quotations marked NCV are taken from the New Century Version®. Copyright © 2005 by Thomas Nelson. Used by permission. All rights reserved. Scripture quotations marked NIV are taken from the Holy Bible, New International Version®, NIV®. Copyright © 1973, 1978, 1984, 2011 by Biblica, Inc.™ Used by permission of Zondervan. All rights reserved worldwide. www.zondervan.com. The "NIV" and "New International Version" are trademarks registered in the United States Patent and Trademark Office by Biblica, Inc.™

No part of this book may be reproduced, stored in a retrieval system, or transmitted by any means without written permission from the author. All rights reserved.

Cover design by: Cornerstone Creative Solutions

For information, address Trilogy Christian Publishing
Rights Department, 2442 Michelle Drive, Tustin, Ca 92780.
Trilogy Christian Publishing/ TBN and colophon are trademarks of Trinity Broadcasting Network.

For information about special discounts for bulk purchases, please contact Trilogy Christian Publishing.

Manufactured in the United States of America

Trilogy Disclaimer: The views and content expressed in this book are those of the author and may not necessarily reflect the views and doctrine of Trilogy Christian Publishing or the Trinity Broadcasting Network.

10 9 8 7 6 5 4 3 2 1

Library of Congress Cataloging-in-Publication Data is available.

ISBN 978-1-63769-374-2 (Print Book)
ISBN 978-1-63769-375-9 (ebook)

PROLOGUE

Recorded History and Context

It is now AD 81. Less than fifty years have passed since Yeshua died. Since the destruction of the Temple almost fourteen years earlier, the members of The Way have now called themselves "Yeshuaians," and their numbers are growing all around the world. However, the Roman authority continues to grow and expand, and much of the wealth stored in the Second Temple has been lost or taken back to Rome for use in Roman public work projects under Vespasian's son, Titus.

Israel is now a separate unit of administration in the eyes of Rome called *Provincia Judaea*. Hebrews speak the name "Israel" amongst themselves, but in the common tongue of Greek, the land in which they live is now called Judah by all. It is a crime to call it by its older name.

Taxes are collected and sent to Rome, but under Titus, Judah's tax burden was reduced. Titus replaced his father Vespasian in AD 79, almost twelve years after sacking Jerusalem and destroying the Second Temple of King Solomon. Although many feared that Titus would be ruthless, he was found to be a great leader and open to new ideas. His reign was short-lived, and he died of what were believed to be natural causes. He was succeeded by his younger brother, Domitian.

Synopsis of Book 1, Behind the Secrets in the Fall of Jerusalem

Yeshua came and left, and the Roman Empire remained in control of Judah. Emperors changed many times after the death of Yeshua, but the Roman power and authority did not. Some people followed the message shared by the Messiah, but most dismissed the stories of His time on the earth, as not all the promises of the prophets had been fulfilled by His deeds while He was living.

Yael, a teenage girl from a Hebrew village in the northern territories of Israel, succumbs to the sin of fornication and decides, on the night of her old sister's wedding, to atone for her sins. She takes minimal supplies and sets out on foot in the middle of the night to reach Jerusalem and make a sacrifice at the Second Temple of King Solomon. According to the Torah, this act of penance will rid her of the guilt and shame caused by her fornication, and she will be able to start life anew and perhaps one day get married to a nice Hebrew man like her sister did.

After viewing unspeakable acts on her six-day journey to the Holy City, she arrives outside the walls of the famed city, only to find the city surrounded and closed off by Roman legions, set on destroying the city as a penalty for defiance against the emperor's claims of authority. The Roman military barred the city gates for three months, allowing no one in or out, as they starved the city into submission. Yael cannot atone for her past without trying to find a way inside, and she sets out in the middle of the night to find a back door entrance. She stumbles upon one of the many hidden tunnels from the days of King David that led into the city and travels underneath it, only to find herself face to face with Mishi, a young rabbi who was building a bunker under the temple to keep the Romans from finding him. She insists that she be allowed to participate in the ritual of atonement to free her of guilt and give her the ability to start life anew, but there are no animals left to sacrifice. The young rabbi cannot help her with her grief but listens to her confession, and the two of them connect. He also confesses that it was sinful for him to hide food and supplies when the people who worked at the Temple school were starving to death. She escapes back out of the city at night, hoping to buy an animal and secretly bring it back into the city using the tunnels and rid herself of the guilt her sin brought upon her.

After she leaves the city through the hidden tunnel she found, she is raped by a Roman guard early one morning. Unknowingly, she becomes pregnant. The same day she is raped, the Romans begin their siege on Jerusalem, and she watches the city and the Temple destroyed.

Back inside the city, Mishi is taken prisoner when the Romans enter the Temple grounds, and he becomes a slave of Rufus. Rufus is the son of the centurion Cornelius from Caesarea and the second in command of the siege. He is a legate, overseeing an entire legion of five thousand Roman soldiers, and he is present during the destruction of the Temple. Rufus engages Mishi and finds the young Jew to be both intellectual and highly social, and Rufus asks him to inquire about what truths may exist in the stories he had heard that there was a new King on the earth named Yeshua. The two of them simultaneously explore the idea together and find evidence that the claims are true.

Meanwhile, an old woman comforts Yael, and she finds her way to the underground synagogue of the followers of

The Way, and she reconnects with Mishi. The two of them are then commissioned by a wounded traveling doctor who had firsthand experience of Yeshua and his follower Paul. The doctor commissions the two of them to transcribe his message, and they make multiple copies to send to the small and floundering churches within the empire. These writings become the book of Luke and the Acts of the Apostles.

As Mishi and Yael work together in the days after the fall of Jerusalem, Mishi falls in love with Yael, even though she is pregnant with another man's child. Although it is unthinkable for a rabbi to marry a woman who is pregnant, he recounts the story of how Yeshua's birth came to pass, and he enters into *erusin*, or engagement, with Yael in a most public manner. Rufus is offered a chance to retire from the Roman military and stay behind, and he takes this opportunity. Once he leaves the Roman military, he has no need for wealth or fame and voluntarily takes a job as Mishi's and Yael's guide and protector. He helps distribute copies of the transcriptions that Yael and Mishi completed, and he escorts them all back to Yael's hometown. Her erusin with Mishi is now complete, and the two of them plan to marry. While there, Mishi tells the village the story of Yeshua, and many are saved. Yael tells her sister that she is pregnant, and her sister tells her that she also is.

Book two, *The Emperor and The Ring*, continues more than thirteen years later when Titus is the emperor, and it is his second year of Roman leadership.

Synopsis of Book 2, The Emperor and the Ring

Yael and Mishi's transcriptions of Luke's words have changed the world, and each of these young leaders is now a sought-after teacher. With Rufus and his men as their guards,

Of Healing and Finding Home

they travel to synagogues around the world to teach the message that Yeshua completes the prophecies of the sacred scrolls. They remain humble yet are viewed as "celebrities" to the established and growing Yeshuaian community. Per the promise Mishi's family made to his community, he and his wife return to Tamar after the fall of the Temple and start a new synagogue and school that includes the teachings of Yeshua. This educational facility is the world's first structure focused on teaching the completed Torah and the fulfillment of Yahweh's promise of a Messiah on the earth. Leaders of the early-based Yeshuaian synagogues send their brightest students and rabbis for tutelage. As the world changed with the destruction of the Temple and Jews dispersed, Yael accepts her place as the Hebrew faith's first female rabbi. She mentors both young women and men with a power of word seldom seen among either men or women.

Yael's raping created a son named Caleb. He is mentored by his adopted uncle Rufus and learns to love hunting, fishing, and tracking. Caleb is physically strong and tall, and he does not look like his father, Mishi. Katya, Yael's sister, also gives birth to a daughter named Eliza. She attends her aunt and uncle's school in Tamar.

Living with her aunt and uncle at night and attending school with them during the day exposes Eliza to the growing Yeshuaian faith in all aspects of life, and Auntie Yael becomes Eliza's childhood hero. Before the start of the next school session, Eliza pleads with her parents to let her make the three-day journey on horseback by herself, even though she is only thirteen years old. Fearing that Eliza might secretly leave her hometown of Correae on her own as her aunt did, her parents allow her to travel to return to school. They also secretly decide to follow behind her a day later to make sure she is safe. When Eliza arrives, she sees her cousin Caleb. See tells him of her trip, and he becomes jealous that she has traveled alone, but he has not yet asked for permission to do so. He asks, and his parents allow the two of them to take an overnight trip to the Philistine city of Kedron for a single night before returning to school.

They return to find Tamar burning and both of Caleb's parents near death. Uncle Rufus was mortally wounded, and the two of them see Eliza's parents enslaved and in chains. In his rage, Caleb kills half of the Roman soldiers in the village, and he kills the centurion in command of their squad. He and Eliza escape before the remaining soldiers mount an offensive and kill them, but they cannot free Eliza's parents before they leave. Eliza promises her parents that they will come back for them.

They travel back to the city they stayed in the previous night and go to the House of Healing. Several trained rabbis help them with the trauma and grief they experience associated with the death and personal loss they witnessed. They are coached as to how to live with their emotions and new identity while maintaining hope for the future. They know that the penalty for killing a Roman soldier, let alone a centurion, is crucifixion, and they choose to unobtrusively travel to Rome to seek an audience with the emperor to ask for his assistance. Caleb took Rufus's military ring off his finger as he died, keeping it to show that he was related to a legate of a Roman legion. His initial plan includes showing that ring to the emperor, reminding him of his childhood friendship with their uncle, and asking for a pardon for his crimes and assistance in finding Eliza's parents. No better plan emerges, and they set out for Rome.

They travel to the port of Joppa and board a sailing vessel bound for Rome. On the first day, a group of three men attempts to rape Eliza. Caleb kills two of them, but the

Of Healing and Finding Home

captain of the ship intervenes and intimidates the only survivor into submission. As they near the Strait of Messina, their boat encounters inclement weather and runs ground. Caleb and Eliza, being prepared, swim to shore with all of their belongings intact. However, most passengers on the boat are lost, and only two others make it to shore with them. One of the survivors is the man who attempted to rape Eliza. She extends grace to him, allowing him to live, thereby tempering Caleb's desire for revenge. Caleb relives the experience of killing as an act of retribution and concludes that it provides him only more pain to endure.

The next day, they discover a small port town near where their boat ran aground and speak to a rabbi at the local synagogue. He gives them a prophecy that has no meaning in the present. They board a new boat and sail into Rome without any other events.

In Rome, they discover that the rumors from Tamar are true, and there are vast numbers of underground synagogues everywhere, despite their proximity to the heart of the Roman Empire. They meet a local rabbi who knew Caleb's parents, and his assistants and synagogue volunteers devise a scheme that affords Eliza and Caleb seats in the royal section of the Colosseum during gladiator fights. The plan works, and they find themselves only two boxed seats away from the emperor. Their box's steward is a slave girl from Judah, only two years older than they are, and she has the same name as Caleb's mother, Yael. They learn that she had listened to Yael teach one time before she was sold into a three-year term as a slave. This new Yael notifies them when Emperor Titus goes to the bathroom, and Caleb walks in on him when he is sitting down on his "throne."

Caleb gives the emperor his uncle's ring and connects the emperor back to his youth. Caleb asks for help, but the emperor, in his perversion, requires Caleb to agree to one of two things: to allow public sexual acts with his cousin Eliza or to watch Caleb fight in the gladiator pits. Caleb is paralyzed but decides that he cannot allow what happened to his mother to happen to his cousin. He acts and angrily agrees to fight in the pits.

He is paired with another warrior, and they must fight two experienced Jewish fighters with 50,000 people watching them. The first to fall in battle is Caleb's partner, and he must now use his experience and his uncle's teachings to kill the two opponents or die and lose his cousin's dignity. He wounds both of his opponents and learns that they are also followers of Yeshua, fighting against their will. Caleb is at a crossroads in his journey to learning the ways of Yeshua and decides to kill his brothers in faith to protect his cousin. As they die, they thank Caleb for ending their earthly existence.

The emperor comes down into the pits to congratulate him, as is Roman custom, and Caleb ponders using his remaining arrow to kill the emperor. He attempts to justify killing the emperor in his mind but instead tosses aside his bow, choosing not to allow his fleshly desire for revenge to lead to a regrettable action. Eliza, with her dignity restored, runs up to Caleb in the view of all at the Colosseum and embraces her cousin. The crowd erupts in joy, seeing what they think are young lovers being reunited.

Eliza boldly offers Caleb's financial reward to the emperor in exchange for the freedom of his servant girl, Yael. Unfamiliar with being publicly spoken to by a woman, the emperor agrees to the terms as the other royalty watch his behavior. The emperor tells them that they must come with him back to the royal palace for what Yael thinks to be an orgy. Upon arrival, they are taken into bathhouses to get readied for the evening's activities, taking luxurious baths, donning oils, and revealing clothing for which they have no choice but to wear.

Caleb is approached by one of the royal houses, soliciting him as a gladiator, offering to pay him the equivalent of half a lifetime's wage for each battle he fights and wins on their behalf. The boy graciously declines this great offer. On the other side of the hallway, the emperor walks into the changing room after Yael and Eliza had finished their preparations. Eliza, filled with the Holy Spirit, presents the story of Yeshua to Titus, and he accepts the truth of Yeshua revealed.

The following morning, servants come into the room that Eliza and Yael spent the night in, offering them a drink that will prevent pregnancy. They both share that the emperor made no advances towards them and they do not need the concoction. They join the emperor on the roof of the palace for breakfast, and he tells them that was the first night he did not have sex since he became the emperor. He asks Eliza to stay and continue as his spiritual teacher and conveys upon her the title of rabbi. She graciously declines his offer to stay and teach him, imploring him to let them return to Judah to save her parents from slavery. He gives her a ring of the Flavian dynasty, thereby equating her with his family in stature throughout the empire. He also gives her a document with the seal of his family on it, requiring anyone with information regarding her parents' whereabouts to release anything they have. She reaches out to a local synagogue, and they agree to send a teacher to the palace each week to instruct the emperor in the ways taught by the Messiah. She also suggests he visit the prisons as the inmates and guards there understand the message of Yeshua. The emperor asks Caleb to return to Rome after his affairs at home are complete, knowing now that Caleb has no family other than Eliza. He suggests that Caleb allow himself to be trained and become a trainer to others in military tactics. Caleb chooses not to reply when he sees that he now has the power to say yes or no. Eliza, like her auntie before her, sees herself becoming a rabbi one day.

After a detour on the way home, they reach Joppa a few days later than expected and learn that the emperor died during their journey back to Judah. Eliza's goods are stolen off the dock, and Yael, the slave who they freed with their bounty from winning in the gladiator pits, and Caleb have an unscripted intimate moment during Eliza's meltdown. After a short stop at the local inn, Caleb decides that they all need to return to the House of Healing, especially Yael. They intend to return to the scene of his crimes in Tamar to begin following the trail of Eliza's parents to set them free.

THE UNANTICIPATED PATH TO SLAVERY

Katya's heart raced, and she whispered prayers of desperation between her whimpers. She had never been to the place of this much need before, and she was scared. She wanted to lean into her husband, as he had always been her emotional rock. Now, his body was being battered by a Roman soldier with ill intent, and he lay pinned to the ground by a knee and the threat posed by an unsheathed sword. He already absorbed several blows to his face and legs, and he now was absorbing their verbal abuse. Her world was crumbling.

She committed to erusin with this man and set herself aside for him and only him, as he met all her family's expectations. He took care of her; he provided for her and their family; he led their family spiritually; he was their healer; he loved them. By his action, he was currently ready to give his life for her, but she knew that there must be another exit from this assault.

But more than the initial act of sacrifice he made to build her a home before receiving permission to marry her, she already knew him to be a very good man. He worked hard, and not just for her. He worked with a focus to preserve the way of life of their village. He was the first to volunteer for projects that helped everyone, and even now, he was trying to plan and finance a road resurfacing project for their hamlet.

It was his love for his wife and their only daughter that brought them here. He agreed to let their daughter travel to school on the other side of their country alone; in retrospect, that choice may have saved her from this conflict. Matthew and Katya did not want their daughter to end up running away in the night like her aunt, rebelling against Hebrew values and culture. Neither of them wanted to see her having children out of wedlock like her hero and his sister-in-law Yael. Yael's act of crossing the country alone some fourteen years earlier resulted in her being raped. Yael gave birth to a child that would never know his biological father. Ironically, it was that same act of leaving home in the middle of the night that led Katya's little sister to meet Rabbi Luke, and she helped to transcribe several scrolls that changed the message of their multi-thousand-year-old faith. Yael became the first female rabbi, and she had since impacted thousands of Jews who looked for a new identity after the fall of Solomon's Temple and the destruction of the greatest artifact of their faith.

One of the Romans grabbed Katya's attention when they struck her cheek with the side of a Roman gladius. Its sting was worse than any force that had ever hit her face. The soldiers told them they were being tried and charged with worshipping a god who claims to be greater than the emperor, and the penalty for this crime was anything the Roman soldier wanted it to be.

Her desperation hit its crescendo. "Yeshua, if you are there, please protect my family!" she spoke out loud, as she had been taught that all prayers must be verbal, and she sobbed as she made her plea to her Messiah.

Of Healing and Finding Home

"Lead us out of this evil moment," she pleaded with Yahweh before pausing, looking for a direction to take her prayer. She was confused after learning a few years earlier that Yeshua was Yahweh's only son. Was she supposed to pray to Yahweh, to His son, or to His Spirit? Apparently, they each had a different role, but she was also told that they were one and the same, and it has always confused her. She was unsure who was the right target for her pleas of desperation, but she committed to throwing the right words to the sky, hoping the right version of Jehovah Jireh would hear her.

"Please forgive us for whatever we did wrong," she said, wiping the tears from her eyes as she watched her husband struck in the face again. The Romans paid no attention to her words; they probably did not speak Hebrew anyway. They continued their pummeling of Matthew, despite Katya's prayers. They spoke to Matthew with a dominant tone that showed their control.

"Hebrew scum! Are you saying this school teaches others that the emperor is not our god?" said the Roman soldier who was striking her husband. He turned his gladius to the broad side and hit Matthew in the shin with a great force. His leg responded by buckling at the knee; she thought it might have broken with that strike. She saw shock was setting in on Matthew, and he had only a few words left before his systems shut down.

"Please, we mean no harm. We came to see our daughter at the Yeshua school," he said, in basic Greek. What he did not know was the second Roman soldier took those words as an admission that the school was meant for those who worshipped Yeshua, and they had heard it said that the followers of Yeshua think him to be greater than the emperor. Their violent response was therefore approved.

"Hebrew scum must learn to comply with Roman law and the emperor's decrees!" the soldier yelled, striking Matthew one more time. Matthew rolled to a different side, trying to protect the damage his front had already absorbed. It was obvious that he was not going to try to fight back with any weapon or word. He was defeated in all ways. Then, the beating stopped, and they stood him up, placing him in chains with his wife.

They were moved in chains from the tree in the village to a cart already filled with children near the village square, away from those still trying to resist. The Roman centurion in charge of this patrol knew that if the children were centralized, the parents would stay and allow themselves to be captured. It was a weakness of a family-centric culture that the Romans knew how to use to their advantage.

Katya had heard of these incidents involving Romans who found Hebrews guilty of worshipping Yahweh or anyone who was not the emperor. She knew the outcome: they would either be killed or taken away and sold or placed into slavery. Questions raced through her mind as she started processing their fate. Would their slavery be temporary or permanent? Would their administrator be cruel or kind? Would he even speak to his slaves, or would he treat them like beasts of burden?

"Yeshua, please keep my daughter safe. Please allow us to see her again. Please give her a long life and give her a venue to serve You. I have poorly served You, as I do not understand You like she does. She loves You and talks to us about You all the time. Give her a way, great Jehovah. Save her, even if You do not save us," she said with her plea, and she repeated it continuously. She knew her faith enough to know that Yahweh is great and can do anything. He had saved her people for thousands of years from repressors. He had sent them a Messiah to free them from the bondage of sin, and there was no force or being that could keep her from Him. He was right there.

But where was He when this absurd event unfolded? Katya and Matthew arrived in the village of Tamar only moments ago, with another group of parents escorting their children to attend her sister's boarding school. With another school session starting in a few days, she and Matthew were one of many families accompanying their children back to Tamar Yeshuaian school. Unlikely circumstance had a group of soldiers on a regional patrol on horseback spot all the activity, and they rode up to the city to see what justified all the action on the roads. When the soldiers arrived, they immediately began asking questions; after all, the flow of people always included the flow of goods, and the flow of goods meant taxation.

An older man and his wife were the grandparents of one of the students, and they spoke up first. They were bringing their granddaughter to the dorms at her school as the parents were too busy. When the patrol asked about the school, they told them in broken Greek that they were delivering their granddaughter to learn about their Yeshua. The old man did not know that this choice of words amounted to criminal behavior, but to publicly acclaim any god other than the emperor was a capital offense. The centurion barked some orders at his soldiers, telling them to separate the group into adults and students. A few of them began setting fires to the school and synagogue, claiming those structures to be blasphemous. Other soldiers started questioning people in smaller groups. When it was Katya and Matthew's turn, the encounter turned violent, quickly. The soldiers never asked them about Eliza, and in the moment, she was grateful that the young girl was not there to see this.

The adults were brought to the village center for questioning. The children were put on a cart and always within visual sight, and the two guards who stood next to the cart of children would attack and kill anyone who attempted to approach it. After a few parents were killed trying to free their children, the others stayed at the distance the Romans commanded.

As the soldiers interviewed a handful of parents, no one denied that the school was teaching the principles of Yeshua in addition to reading, writing, mathematics, Jewish history, and Jewish culture. The centurion did not want conflict, and he offered a compromise. He told them all that could take their children and leave, with a sworn commitment never to return nor teach to their children of this blasphemy. The Romans had learned years ago that Jews took sworn commitments with them for generations; sworn oaths were found to be the best tool to invoke a change in behavior with Hebrews.

None of the parents took the Roman centurion up on his offer of freedom in exchange for discarding the practice of their faith, and the Roman leader became livid. The oldest man who was the first to say no was struck down by a single swing of a Roman blade, screaming as he died. All the noise caused Yael and Mishi to step out from their home adjacent to the synagogue and school. They saw that the school and synagogue were burning. Mishi attempted to engage them in dialog, as he knew two of the soldiers. At the centurion's command, he was stabbed with a javelin by a soldier on horseback, who mortally wounded him. Yael stepped between the soldier and her stabbed husband, commanding them to stop in the name of Yeshua. With that, the Romans left their horses and swung a gladius at Yael. She raised her arm to protect herself, and the sharp blade went through her arm, cutting it off above the hand. Several other parents who were watching fell to their knees, vomiting at the sight of the atrocity. The soldier then swung his weapon at Yael a second time, killing her. Yael never saw that her older sister and brother-in-law had arrived, as their daughter told her yesterday that she came alone. No one was expecting Katya and Matthew.

The soldier yelled out, "Who else wants to step in front of our blades for their false faith?" and with that, Rufus stepped forward. He had been working in the stables and wore no armor nor held any weapons other than a wooden rake—he was unprepared for combat. He attempted to talk to them, but three of the soldiers engaged him in melee, each from a different direction. Their training and advantage of numbers overtook all of his years of training and lack of a suitable weapon, and two of the three connected with Rufus's flesh with their attacks. Rufus could only parry one of their assaults, and he was quick to fall from his wounds.

In a flash, the tide of the moment changed. Caleb arrived, dashing out from a corner of the village square, and surprised the Roman soldiers. His passion for defending his family and community was unleased, and the training of Caleb's uncle Rufus was his primary tool. He immediately killed several Roman soldiers with his bowmanship skills. The centurion tried to flank him, but Caleb kept his poise and thoughtfully carved up the battle test soldier using his wits more than his weapons. Caleb was able to defeat a man with more years of combat experience than Caleb had been on this earth. All the while, Katya prayed for Caleb to have supernatural alertness as he rounded the corner where the centurion set his trap. When her prayers appeared to be answered, Caleb made eye contact with Katya and Matthew.

Katya continued her prayers with fervor, perceiving that they were getting answered.

"Yeshua, empower our nephew with the strength to save us all. Protect him from harm and take care of my daughter!"

It seemed like there would be no end to her pleas this day.

She looked up, and the remaining Romans were now focused on Caleb. From the right side of her field of vision, she saw a blur moving towards her quickly. Before the moment was halfway passed, Eliza stood next to her mother, panting and sweating.

"Mother, mother! What is happening here?"

"These soldiers are enslaving us. They think that this school exists to create blasphemy against the emperor," Katya whispered. This was the first instance she discovered that her face was swollen from the impact of the blows, as it was difficult to open her mouth.

"We will get you out of this mess," said Eliza.

"Are you safe, Little One?" asked her mother.

"Yes, of course," she said.

"Good. Yes, Good. I am glad you were not with us when we arrived," said Katya.

"Mother, I arrived here yesterday. The Romans do not know who we are. We will return and find you, okay?"

As her daughter finished the last words, they both heard Caleb engaging in loud verbal exchanges with the remaining Roman soldiers, and she knew that they would soon organize and hunt him down as they were on horseback. That meant they would be hunting down Eliza, too.

"Go, Little One!" Katya whispered with earnest to her daughter and nodded her head emphatically to get her out of danger. Her daughter turned and ran out of the village center, never detected by the Romans. Caleb also ran that way, and Katya watched him grab Eliza's hand and leave the village when they were out of sight of the remaining soldiers.

Of Healing and Finding Home

The soldiers spoke amongst themselves. Moments later, the children were unloaded, and the adults were placed on the cart instead. One of the parents was put in charge of driving the cart after being struck a few times and given orders not to speak. The wagon immediately left Tamar and headed east on the road towards Jerusalem. The body of the dead centurion was thrown in the cart with them.

Katya knew where they were going. She had heard the stories. Their life was now forfeit. They were to be slaves, property of the Roman Empire, most likely working on making Jerusalem into a more Roman city.

THE LIFE OF A ROMAN SOLDIER IN JUDAH

The Roman soldiers seemed very satisfied to complete their vision of Hebrew behavior modification. Permission to beat and rape Jews who did not do what was asked of them was one of the few carnal pleasures that soldiers were allowed to experience while living and working in foreign lands on assignment for the empire. Almost none of the soldiers wanted to be in Judah; indeed, they hated it. The soldiers missed their homes, and they hated that the empire required that they live so far from family and their homes. Some petitioned their administrators and centurions to allow them to serve in Gaul; others asked for posts in nearby Sicilia or Calabria. Judah was considered a lousy assignment. Even Egypt was a better assignment, as traveling home on holiday was shorter and safer. Being sent to Judah was the punch line of jokes within the military.

Yet, for most Romans, serving in the military was a well-paying job with many perks. They often received booty from their pillaging, and in some instances, they would be granted land and slaves after a conquest if they chose to stay and serve as a local official. There was a pension for those who lived long enough to retire, and a plot of land of considerable size was given to all who lasted ten years. Yet, few soldiers ever stayed in Judah. It was hot and arid, and it was a long way from civilization, as far as they were concerned.

Roman soldiers universally hated the Jewish resistance. For their efforts to serve the empire, the Hebrew constituents threw rocks at the soldiers. They placed pit traps on the roads they used. They poisoned their food and tainted their water by mixing it with urine. Titus understood their plight, as he once served for a season outside of Jerusalem. He led the siege on the city, destroying the Temple and pillaging the city's precious metals and artwork. He sent much of that back home, where it was used for public works projects. As such, Titus sided with the perceived needs of the soldiers, for he knew how lonely life in a foreign land could be. The emperor camped in front of the City of David, treating Hebrew women as carnal flesh through three months of boredom. His soldiers could not afford to purchase a whore every night, nor were there enough whores for all of his men. He empathized with their pain and extended them any freedom he could imagine, including no consequences for poorly treating the residents of Judah.

Many Roman soldiers had wives and children, but not all. To make it easy, there was a ration of coin given to each centurion to keep his soldiers full of wine and afford an occasional woman. For most, those were the only items of interest that the soldiers looked forward to each day.

Titus issued a decree that allowed any soldier who was assaulted by a Hebrew to independently enforce any penalty that he deemed appropriate, so long as at least two other soldiers were present when the act occurred. With a total of ten of them present when the husband-and-wife rabbis claimed Yeshua to be the Messiah, they were formally authorized to do anything that they wanted as part of the "Roman Consequence," for blasphemy.

Of Healing and Finding Home

And these facts about the life of Roman soldiers serving in Judah are what made some of them interested in the freedom associated with getting to know a loving Messiah.

JEALOUS ELIZA

Eliza stood on the outer porch of the inn in Joppa, feeling numb. They had a late breakfast as teenagers tend to do, and it was time to start the trip inland to Yael's home. Caleb and Yael tried to lift up her spirits, but she was not talking to either of them. The three of them had been sailing for about two weeks, and both Yael and Caleb thought Eliza should be ecstatic that they were on home soil. They had a stop in Messina for a few days while they waited out some bad weather, but they were told to expect that.

    Caleb sustained no wounds during his time in the Colosseum pits when he fought against two combatants, but his soul was wounded from slitting the throats of two followers of Yeshua. How many people now had Caleb killed? He killed four or five Roman soldiers in Tamar when they attacked his family. He killed two on the boat for attempting to rape Eliza. He killed two Yeshua followers in the Colosseum pits, with 50,000 people cheering for death. At least he restrained himself and did not try to kill the emperor. When would the requirements to kill stop? Were these even requirements?

    Despite these haunting scars from what transpired in the Colosseum, they all had a good night's rest and had good food in their bellies. They had talked about how wonderful the first night's sleep on dry land would be, and it did not disappoint. The Jewish spices and tea with camel milk were exactly what they hoped it would be, and at least two of the three of them were feeling positive.

They were finally ready to begin the next stage of their adventure and get Yael back home. Caleb took a few of Eliza's coins and stocked their wagon with fresh bread, vegetables from the market, fruit, and all their remaining luggage from the trip. Yael was full of excitement and joy, as she was almost home, and this was a dreamlike moment for her that she had hoped for. Yet, joy was blatantly absent from Eliza's face.

She tried to snap herself out of it by taking a gratitude check. Aunt Yael taught her that when life seems horrible, you should look to see all the good that exists and use that to replace the bad that you see. Eliza looked down at her left hand. On her middle finger sat a gift from the emperor that publicly displayed and granted Eliza's place in the House of Flavian and immunity from Roman regulations. Its worth was far above the value of the metals, gems, and workmanship. When she wore it, she was viewed as a family both to the last emperor and the present one, making her perhaps the most powerful and influential Hebrew currently alive on the earth. She took a moment to think only about that as she took ten deep breaths. In addition to exemption from literally every Roman law, her village had immense wealth from their treasury of gold ore. She thanked Yahweh for providing for her in ways that few in all of recorded history could understand. Literally, no citizen of Correae ever went without material possessions for any extended period. Eliza, Caleb, and Yael could afford anything for sale within the empire. She took ten breaths and embraced that reality.

It made no earthly sense that she should be depressed. Granted, her parents had been taken into slavery, but she had been given enough tools and enough hope to think that she,

Yael, and Caleb should be able to find them and see them set free.

Before she finished the last of her gratitude and breathing exercises, she could see more clearly some of the sources of her discontent. Titus's death changed Eliza. She was mourning his loss. Yet, there was more there. When she learned that Caleb had intentions of exploring a greater relationship with Yael, Eliza went from a state of sadness to depression. Yael was her friend, first. Her conversations with Yael on the boat ride home were nearly as intimate as the ones her parents would share. She and Yael also connected at a most intimate level, as Yael disclosed all of her pent-up feelings associated with the multiple sexual assaults she endured. Yael was supposed to be her Hebrew sister, and two teenage girls were supposed to be closer than a teenage boy and a teenage girl. It had always been that way in Judah. Yet, she saw that Caleb was interested in girls, and this is the way of things. He was the son of Hebrew royalty, beautiful and powerful enough to have anyone he wanted. Yet, Caleb decided to pick a common girl without a royal background who happened to be the most important girl in Eliza's life. Why couldn't he pick someone else or wait till he got back home to start searching for a life partner? Her feelings were hurt, and she was jealous.

She thought about giving him her ring if he and Yael would just be friends. But that effort would be useless. Caleb already had a ring himself, signifying that their uncle was a legate in the military. Uncle Rufus used to command five thousand men, and Caleb was his nephew. The emperor told Caleb that if he conducted himself the way he always did and showed that ring, any of the members of the military would listen to him and do what he would tell them. It was as if Caleb, too, was a member of a royal household. He did not need Eliza's ring; perhaps he no longer needed her if he had Yael. She felt alone and unneeded.

"Eliza, please, tell me what is wrong?" pleaded Yael. Caleb had already gone to place all of the items that they brought home from Rome in the cart and speak with their driver. He was arranging their gear so two could ride in the cart with the gear and driver while one of them walked. They agreed to take turns walking.

"I do not know," Eliza said, failing to look at Yael.

She then looked at Yael and exhaled a chuckle. "I think I am jealous of you and Caleb," she said.

"You are stupid!" said Yael. She had heard Caleb say that to her more than once, and it seemed to fit the moment. "That is total nonsense."

"I do not want to lose you, either of you," she said.

"Why would you lose us?" asked Caleb. He had finished what he needed to do and walked up behind them and heard the last piece of their conversation.

Neither of them answered him.

"What is it?" Caleb asked again. They both knew it was disrespectful to ignore a Hebrew male's question. Their lack of response revealed that this was a real issue. After another moment of quiet, Caleb gave up and moved on.

"Eliza, I found the two bags you thought were stolen. One of the porters had put it on a different cart. The cart owner was still by the port, and I saw them. Everything was still there, even all the coin you got from the cinnamon sale proceeds," he said.

Eliza stood up, walked to Caleb, and embraced him. It was awkward, and Caleb took a moment to respond and reciprocate. She then pushed him back for a moment and looked him in the eyes.

"I am jealous of your feelings towards Yael. I love her, and I love you, but it makes me feel alone to see you connect with Yael. And I know that I need both of you," she said.

"Well, you aren't going to be alone anytime soon. We are going to spend every moment together today on this rinky-dink cart I wished I had not hired as we travel to Gezer." Gezer was Yael's hometown, and they might reach it by midafternoon, pending no unanticipated problems.

Caleb carried the last of the girls' stuff and put it in the wagon, and the two girls got in the cart to ride first. Caleb walked next to them, as this section of the road into and out of Joppa was wide enough to support the cart and him without leaving the road. Once they left the metropolitan Joppa area, Caleb was relegated to walk behind the cart.

The first part of the day was uneventful, but the cart broke as they neared a small town, and the cart owner said he needed to walk to the small village nearby to get some iron to fix one of the wheels. He was only a few steps from the group when Yael spoke up, asking the cart owner to stop for a moment.

"Why don't the two of you walk ahead with the cart owner? I will watch the gear, and you two can get some tea until the cart gets fixed and we meet you." She wanted to give them time together.

"Not a chance," said Caleb. "You two go with him, and I will stay here and watch the cart. There was a game trail next to the road right behind us, and I might go for a hunt. The wind speed is really low now, and there are a lot of clouds in the sky. My odds are better than good that I will have some success. Wouldn't some fresh game taste good?" he asked.

They paused for a second, then he extended his bow towards Eliza and spoke again, "Unless, of course, you want to stay here and watch the cart alone and deal with any marauders who happen to come by," he said.

"Okay, we get it," said Eliza as she rolled her eyes and left with Yael. Caleb could care less about petty jealousy. He lived for unprompted hunting moments like these. He put his new Roman bow and quiver of perfectly shafted arrows over his shoulder and walked back towards where they came. The girls walked towards the small town they could see in the distance that the driver was going to.

Eliza opened up about how hearing of the loss of Titus impacted her. She had spent much of her quiet time thinking about and praying for him while they were on the boat. To learn that he was dead was a unique loss, as he was the first adult whom she had ever presented the gospel of Yeshua. She felt empty that he was gone. She did exactly what her aunt told her to do, and she saw it blossom. Then, he was taken away by what everyone believed were natural causes. Eliza knew that it was a spiritual event that took his life, and she was grieving. She had imagined how Emperor Titus would change the world as a follower of Yeshua. Laws and decrees would come to pass that changed the world for the better. She opened up and told Yael that she fantasized that all slavery would come to an end and her parents would be free. She daydreamed that all rulers everywhere would become loved by the people they served, and there would be no more fear of authority. She prayed that her village would be freed of the burden of secrecy associated with operating a hidden vein of gold, but she did not tell about the gold mine in Correae— she still had no right to disclose that information.

When she had finished talking, the cart owner was already on his way back to the cart, as he found the size and shape of iron that he needed as soon as they met with the village blacksmith.

"So, that is what has occupied my heart," Eliza said.

For her part, Yael had been listening.

"You know, I knew Titus before you did, and I had seen him do some horrible things to women, but he never did them to me, nor did he do them to his concubine. He knew both of us were Hebrew, as well. When we left, my hope was that he would stop doing all of those things and that the fights in the gladiator pits would stop forever. You know, I think it was Rufus's investment in his childhood friend after he became a Yeshua follower that started the changes in his heart. I see no other reason for him to have left me undefiled. That was not his nature," she added.

"Yeah, I had that thought, too," said Eliza.

Eliza felt a moment of sorrow as the words that Yael just used reminded her of a story that her aunt would tell all the children during their early days of middle school. The world sought hope from the oppression that the Romans currently posed to the Hebrew faith. The sacred scrolls made mention repeatedly of a Messiah who would save them from evil men and the enslavement that was inseparable from the Roman Empire. They did not understand that the Messiah was meant to save them from the evil of their own hearts and their tendency to sin. They never saw that their heart was the greatest enemy of their people. Sinners were not the problem. Sin was.

For his part, Eliza's uncle Mishi would share alongside his wife. He would tell tales from his school days when he lived and studied on the Temple grounds. The Pharisees above him told them all of a promise that one day, Yahweh would send a Messiah to save them from all the oppression, and they taught all the children to go to the Temple and offer prayers that Yahweh honor His promises. It wasn't until they became friends with Luke that they learned that Yeshua had already come.

As the girls discussed what might have come to pass had Titus lived, they agreed that the emperor could not make people worship Yeshua; individuals make that choice independent of their government. Choosing Yeshua was not a script to be followed nor ancient teaching that required deep instruction to understand. Emperor Titus understood the message in a fraction of an evening, but it would not be from the heart of Yahweh if he issued an edict that everyone had to follow this new teaching. Now that Titus was dead and his brother Domitian was the emperor, all things with faith were reset. The girls agreed that they needed to pray for Domitian as much as they did for Titus.

"Maybe one day in the future, there will be another emperor who accepts Yeshua as the Messiah and tries to make things right between Yahweh and His people. I just hope it happens in less than a thousand years or something," they halfheartedly prayed in chorus.

When they got back to the cart, they saw that Caleb had killed a deer, and he was positioning it on the cart. Eliza went to Caleb to congratulate and affirm his skill as a hunter. Both girls had talked about how much affirmation impacted Caleb, especially now that both of his parents and his favorite uncle were gone. Yael replicated Eliza's efforts, and Caleb thanked both of them before reiterating his desire to eat fresh kill. The cart owner had them underway quickly, and he felt confident they would still reach Gezer that day.

They all had to walk behind the cart for the rest of the day, so they all got to talk and play. They got to do this on the boat ride home, as well. It felt good to be kids again.

Eliza and Caleb extended to Yael much more than sisterhood, words, and a story. They purchased her freedom back using all of Caleb's earnings for winning the gladiator fight. Yael had been sold into slavery by her family and indentured to serve in Rome for a term of three years. Her family needed the coin to survive, and they felt that there was no other choice to keep their family intact without the oldest daughter "working" in Rome temporarily. They told her it would be like military service. It was not. She dressed up nicely and served many of the Roman elite, but she was not treated like a human. Indeed, she was abused. Now, she would be coming home to see if the sacrifices were worth it.

ARRIVING IN GEZER

As they got closer to Gezer, it was obvious that Yael was nervous. She continually checked her clothes and her hair, trying to look the best she could before her big reveal and arrival. She made sure that her purse of coins was on her outer garments, as she intended to give it to her father as soon as they reached the inside of their home. Based on the height of the sun, it appeared that they would be arriving late afternoon, so everyone should have come back to the village after performing the tasks associated with a late winter work cycle.

"Almost there," said Yael, albeit with a sense of fear and anxiety as they were within an arrow's shot of the village perimeter. For her part, Eliza wanted to make a good impression on Yael's parents. She put some saliva on her fingertips and used it to keep back part of her dark hair as well as clean her nose and chin area. Every Hebrew girl learned this act of cleaning before entering a place of importance. Although nowhere in the sacred scrolls does it say that cleanliness is part of the heart of Yahweh, it was inferred and practiced throughout all of Judah. Caleb found it a bit amusing watching how sensitive the girls were to the perception of judgment that was coming their way.

As soon as they reached the hamlet's edge, Caleb and Eliza were saddened to see how destitute the village and its residents appeared. The roads in and out of town were not maintained by either the village leadership or the Roman public works division. There were multiple ruts on each side of the road, and there were large potholes on the main road coming in from the west. The ride was bumpier than it should have been based on the time of the year. Normally, villagers come together and smooth all roads in and out, as well as repair any holes that formed after the harvest season and the rainy season. Those seasons ended three months ago. In a normal village, the last half league of travel should have been a blend of Roman cobbles and brick, resistant to the effects of bad weather and erosion. Those construction elements also create noises when the hooves of an animal or the wheels of a cart pass. Any traveler would be heard long before they were seen, providing a level of safety for the residents.

There should also have been a shrubbery on each side of the road, as well, keeping the larger beasts of burden from crossing the road at undesignated places. Lastly, there should have been some sort of entryway or manmade arch as travelers and visitors crossed into the center of the village. This decoration of the entry into the village would create a stronger and more unique memory of the time spent there. The village square was the place where the village patriarchs and people spent their time when they were not farming or attending to their business. There was no such monolith that gave Gezer any identity. Even the manger in the center of town for visiting beasts of burden was run down and appeared not to have been emptied in weeks. It smelled horrible.

Caleb and Eliza had both seen this type of run-down and unmaintained Hebrew village in the past, but they did not ask Yael what happened. Yael had been gone over a year, and she would not know why, but they could see the shame on Yael's face as they entered. They all knew that a village in this condition meant that the residents had lost their sense of pride. This was a bad look for its residents and the Hebrew folks who passed through here.

As they reached the center of the village, Yael told the cart owner to stop. The only people in the village center were a few children playing outside; there were no adults to be found. There were animals walking all over the village square, and their excrement was everywhere. Where was the shepherd in charge of the flocks today?

"I am sorry you had to see this. Something has happened here," said Yael, obviously shamed by this public display.

Yael jumped off the cart and turned back to Caleb and Eliza.

"Please wait here. I am going to get my father," she said. She ran towards her childhood home, assuming that everyone would be pleased to have her back. She entered a house near the northeast corner of the square as Caleb and Eliza watched and waited.

Both Caleb and Eliza expected to wait only moments before the Hebrew family emerged from their home, inviting them into their house for a meal and a celebration. Yael did return immediately, but instead of joy and invitations, she came out of her house with tears flowing from her eyes. Eliza jumped out of the cart and ran towards her distressed friend while Caleb stood up in the cart and watched.

"What is it, what is it?" said Eliza, in a loving tone.

Yael tried to stop crying and wipe the tears from her eyes.

"My little sister, Hannah," and she paused as deep sobs began to shake her. No one else was in the village square, and it seemed odd that they were alone right now.

"What?" said Eliza as she placed both of her hands on Yael's shoulders.

"He sold her, too. Or, at least, she is gone!" she said, finally allowing the overwhelming force of this new trauma overcome her. She began crying uncontrollably.

From her house emerged a middle-aged Jew wearing no shirt or sandals. He was normal-sized in stature. He should not be dressed this way, especially at this time of day; Caleb knew that all Hebrew men should be working during the times that the sun is up.

He yelled out as he left the entryway of his family's small home using very diminutive terms, thinking no one was listening.

"And all you brought back from Rome was this coin? What am I going to do with this scrawny amount, you piece of dung!" he said, holding up Yael's coin purse.

Caleb had seen enough. He quickly reached into the bag of goods he brought home from Rome and unsheathed the celebratory gladius that Titus had given him as a commemoration of winning a battle in the Colosseum against multiple opponents. It was ornate but too clumsy to be used as a combat weapon, but it would suffice to perform the act he intended. It was made of polished steel and had never seen combat. The blade was wide and reflected the afternoon sun like a mirror.

His next move was one from Uncle Rufus's repertoire of tactics for dealing with individuals who were out of line. Although he had used this Roman tool of forced submission, his uncle had shown him how, and Caleb had practiced it with his uncle more than once.

He jumped down and briskly walked towards Yael's father, with the blade held so that the hilt was at chest level and the sword was overhead so that the person about to be threatened could see the width of the blade. The blade's position above the head of the opponent also created a sense of submission as the only direction that it could travel was down, and the opponent would innately conclude that it was going to come down with the sole intent of striking them.

Once Caleb got within ten steps, he spoke using the tone that Rufus had taught him to use, followed by a repetition of the same words at a higher volume, to ensure the recipient of his wrath complied with his demands.

"On your knees or die this very day," he said, unwavering in his steps. Yael's father lost all focus on his daughter and stared at the stranger and his weapon.

Eliza, for her part, had no idea that Caleb was composed. She assumed pure rage was flowing in his veins. She had seen him kill Roman soldiers in his rage as well as kill men to protect her. She had also seen him risk his life to protect her and Yael. Now that he had expressed affection for Yael and had openly discussed a relationship, she thought he might kill again, this time to protect her honor. She did not know that Caleb had been taught to do this act. She thought he was reacting to Yael's pain with an overreaction of his own.

"Caleb! *No!*" she yelled. She maintained her grip on Yael, pulling her close so she would not have to see the probable death of her father. Her trust in Caleb was under assault, and she was not ready for another moment of loss.

Caleb increased his volume as he spoke to this now diminished man, making sure that he could see the size and width of his sword as he raised his elbow to the level of his mouth.

"On your knees or die this very day!" he repeated.

Just as Rufus told him it would happen, the man fell to his knees, dropping everything in his hands. Despite the presence of the sword, Yael's father looked Caleb in the eye.

Uncle Rufus told him that once he initiated these acts of aggression and dominance against an individual, his dominating stature would create an outcome that the Romans learned was as predictable as the sunrise. His uncle's teachings came to life in this moment, and he heard his uncle speaking to him.

"Caleb, when that man drops to his knees in compliance with your threat, you have a singular moment to control some of the outcomes in their life. Of course, you can swing your weapon; but you will have other options that represent even greater power. However, they require self-control to harness. These are the skills you must learn, and they are more difficult to learn than the skills needed to kill a man."

Caleb had seen enough poor behavior from this man to know he did not deserve his daughter. Yael had spoken about coming home to her family with great joy. She would be a year earlier than expected, and she anticipated that they would rejoice and celebrate together. She had been counting the days since the morning they left the emperor's palace in Rome less than three weeks ago. She deserved a father who loved her and felt sorrow for selling her into slavery.

More of his uncle's words returned to his thoughts.

"You can pronounce judgment on the man kneeling before you, perhaps sentencing him to great amounts of suffering, with no fear of retribution or violent response. This is the human temptation, and I saw my father teeter and fall with a decision he made when I was five years old. There was a man caught stealing bread for his family a second time. My father had already tried him once and had threatened him publicly that the next time he committed this crime, he would kill him. My father did not hesitate; he took out his gladius and beheaded the man with his family watching."

Rufus stood up and walked to the edge of the fire ring as he told Caleb this story.

Of Healing and Finding Home

"That evening, he told me that the worst thing he did was to tell that man that if he did it again, he would kill him. He wished he had provided better guidance than a threat. When possible, pick a route that includes speaking into the man's heart. That way, you will find it easier to sleep at night. Point out to him what it is that he cannot see. Speak to him what he cannot hear otherwise. It is in these moments that his heart and his senses will be most receptive." The two of them were tracking a herd of mountain goats when Rufus told him that story. Caleb will never forget the day Rufus shared that with him.

Rufus warned Caleb of the consequences of abusing this power.

"Caleb, your authority will drive you mad if you misuse it. Issue no edict and do no act that will prevent you from sleeping well that night. Kill only when you have no other choice," his uncle would tell him.

And with that, Caleb spoke. However, he focused on his choice of verbs. Rufus told him they were more powerful than nouns during these moments. He lowered his blade to waist level, removing a portion of the perceived threat.

"You have sold your oldest daughter into slavery, and she returns to you earlier than her term of service, and you disgrace her with this public display of vulgar words and a lack of gratitude. What say you to these charges?" he made sure that his last question was spoken with greater volume than the charges. He was taught that this ensures no delay in answer.

"My daughter! Please do not kill me. Please do not kill my daughter!" he repeated.

"No! Don't kill him!" said Yael, yelling and sobbing. Both girls were now watching Caleb as he stood over the Hebrew man with a gladius poised to kill. Both girls knew

43

Caleb capable of swinging the blade, but both girls also knew Caleb to be held captive by the scars left on his soul by other equally justified killings. Both men in their field of view were at a crossroads, and no one, including Caleb, knew how this would end. Neither girl had any idea what he was about to do, but they had to trust him. He had risked his life for them three weeks earlier, and he had earned their trust.

Caleb stood over the pathetic man and felt the meaning of his uncle's words. He felt power soar in his blood. In that first moment of wielding this power, he loved this feeling. His desire to make an example of this man was as real as hunger at the end of a fall day of hunting. Yet, he could not dismiss any of his uncle's or his parents' teachings in these moments. He was experiencing turmoil as to how to proceed.

In this moment of crisis, he began to feel that an overlay of his mother's words approached upon his uncle's teachings. She taught him that Yeshua gives second chances. She was one of His second chances. He was one of Yeshua's second chances. Every man deserved a second chance. Balbi was given a second chance that he did not deserve. Caleb stood there, wondering what his next move should be. How should he extend to this man a second chance?

The man began to cry. Caleb expected this. He might have also relieved himself in his loin. Uncle Rufus told him that this was also common. His tears fueled Caleb's sense of power. However, it provided Caleb no guidance as to what to do next.

He smiled as the answer came to him. Caleb remembered that he chose to give the emperor a second chance when he discarded his bow from the Colosseum and did not shoot the emperor at point-blank range. That very day, Eliza presented the gospel of Yeshua to Titus, and he listened and learned. None of that would have happened had Caleb not extended the grace his mother taught him that everyone deserved.

"Why did you commit such a heinous crime as to let your daughter be taken without a fight?" Caleb asked, this time with a calm tone. He knew to alternate tones to achieve control of the situation.

"My wife. She died. We had nothing, my son and me. I needed to preserve my son to preserve our family line, so he stayed here with me," he said before he also began crying uncontrollably. Sons were more important in Hebrew culture, and Caleb knew that. If a man felt forced into that decision, he would not be found guilty of choosing to protect his son over his daughter.

"Please don't kill my daughter. Don't kill my daughter! I have dreamed of her coming home for so long!" he said between sobs.

Caleb had no intention of killing anyone. He already heard from Yael over the last three weeks as they sailed from Rome that their entire village was already poor before she was sold into slavery. Marauders had come in and taken their harvest only the day before taxes were due. Many of the residents of the village sold their children into slavery the same day that she was sold to pay the taxes, but they did not get enough to replace the loss of the year's grains.

Caleb threw his sword into the distance and yelled. Then, he approached the man and stood him up. Caleb was much stronger than this man, and there was no need to continue with this show of dominance. Caleb would win no matter what path they took next. There was no need to create distance with this man when he needed an emotional gap to be bridged.

"You have had some bad luck, Uncle," he said, honoring the man with a title reserved for family and close teachers. Yael and Eliza also stopped holding each other tightly and watched the next exchange with a heightened awareness of the words to be spoken. Caleb towered over the man and looked down on him. The man continued to look at the ground, feeling shame. Caleb then sat down next to the man, crossed legged and put his hands on his knees. He looked into his eyes and spoke.

"Your daughter deserves better than what you just did to her and all of us! You must be told what she has done since you sold her. It is a horror that I require you to endure. It is fair," Caleb said. Neither of the girls could tell if he was serious with his comment or not. Caleb decided that it is in this way that he will exercise his once-in-a-lifetime authority over this man.

"Uncle, what is your name?" he asked.

"It is Zevdorr," he said. "People call me 'Zev.'" Caleb could already tell this man was having a difficult time adjusting to their relationship's change in authority. Caleb was returning to the culture of verbally treating the elderly as superior and worthy of honor. He already felt that he should be apologizing to Uncle Zev.

"I am called Caleb, and my parents were both killed only last month. I have killed many people in this time, and I killed no less than two men protecting your daughter's honor. I am sorry; I meant you no harm, Uncle, but your behavior made me want to kill you. Come and sit with me," pausing long enough for its impact to settle in. He was trained by one of the best teachers in how to use empty gaps of time to make an impact.

Two other men came out from their homes to watch the screaming and saw the swordsman. Caleb knew that he had their attention as well. He turned to them and gave them instructions.

Of Healing and Finding Home

"Take the deer from the back of our cart and cook it. Serve the entire village with it. Make haste," he said. He gestured for the men to fetch the deer, and they immediately left, shouting orders to their families to begin lighting fires in the village pits. Others came out to help, and the village slowly came to life as the offer of free, fresh game gathered everyone's attention.

Over the next window of time, everyone watched as other villagers came out and did what Caleb told them to. Some began cleaning up the animal waste. Others began picking up debris on the road, and others ran out to the fields to tell everyone to come home to celebrate the return of a prodigal daughter. When the mayor approached Caleb, Caleb greeted him with honor and told him everything that had just transpired. The mayor nodded and told Caleb that he would personally take stewardship of the rest of the village meal's preparation.

Caleb took off his shoes as a sign of respect and spoke to Zev.

"But even if you do not treat her as our forefathers have taught us to treat the women in our families, I will, Uncle."

And with that, the moment to impact the man's heart had passed. What came next was not part of Caleb's training.

The man, for his part, sat back on his feet and stopped his crying. Caleb motioned for Yael to come forward, and Caleb owned the flow of the conversation. The authority that came from his previous act also passed through to Yael and Eliza, and both of them were scared of Caleb. Uncle Rufus told him how his mother would be scared of his father when he would do similar things, but it was now upon him to act like a gentleman to keep their respect.

While the villagers prepared and cooked the deer, Caleb, Yael, Zev, and Eliza sat by themselves at the edge of the village square. A few girls of the same age as Eliza and Yael stood within hearing distance, but they also feared Caleb and did not approach him any further.

The conversation began as everyone started revealing what had transpired in the last year and a half. After Yael left with the slave traders, Zev received two and a half years of wages in exchange for three years of service to the empire. The slavers kept six months of Yael's labor as their fee. Zev paid the taxes due to the Romans and all his outstanding debt and had some extra money. Unfortunately, his wife got sepsis and died less than a week after Yael left, and the village could not find him another bride. He used over half of his remaining coin to purchase an affordable slave. The elderly woman was helpful, but she died within six months. Without a wife, slaves, or any children old enough to work the field, he lost the ability to maintain their farm.

Zev took his son and daughter and traveled to a nearby village where his dead wife's cousin lived as he was looking for a place to keep them safe while he set out to find a new wife. He decided that without a woman, the life of a Hebrew man was incomplete.

After he dropped off his children, he returned to Gezer to get some affairs in order. He learned that his cousin's village was raided the following day, and his son and daughter were taken. He abandoned his efforts to find a new bride and spent nearly all of his coin searching for his two remaining children. During bouts of uncontrollable tears, he told Yael, Caleb, and Eliza how others in the village had similar experiences. Before he finished his story, several other village members with similar stories had come out and sat with Zev as he finished his.

"This was a great evil. None should ever have to experience this. Roman occupation is the greatest bane of our people's history, I tell you now. There is no way that our captivity during the time of Nebuchadnezzar was this evil," he said, crying in front of his daughter with greater tears than she had ever seen him cry. He attempted to cover his face as the tears fell, but he had nothing other than his arm; instead, he bowed his head, and everyone watched the tears fall onto his lap.

"I tell you, we were hopeless, yes, beyond hope. During these times, I could not find a new wife, but I desperately needed one. I missed your mother more than words can express!" he said, looking up at Yael almost like a puppy looks at its mother.

Caleb knew that his role had just shifted from that of a judge to that of a healer. His father routinely told him this and demonstrated to him how to display the traits of a healer. For his part, Caleb gestured for both Yael and Eliza to come and sit with Zev. Yael held him and cried with him throughout his tale. As he neared the end of it, he looked at his daughter in her eyes and spoke words that Caleb knew would come. In fact, these were the words that justified all of his actions that day.

"My precious daughter, it is true that hurt people hurt people. I am ashamed of how I treated you this day. You are all that I have. I am so sorry," he said, ending his apology with what everyone agreed was sincere remorse as he placed his head on Yael's shoulder, allowing her to comfort him.

Eliza looked at Caleb, seeking some guidance. It was inappropriate for any woman other than family to touch a man in public. Yet, everyone knew that Zev needed all the family he could get in this moment. Caleb gestured for her to embrace the man on the opposite side of Yael as if he were her family. She moved slowly but complied. Zev was too emotional to be aware of Eliza's presence; he accepted the affection she offered without comment. The friends of Yael's who had been watching in the distance were riveted to the embrace and sharing in this scene, and they spoke amongst themselves; Caleb did not know what they said. He gestured for them to come and sit with them as well, and they ran forward, sitting next to their friend and holding on to each other.

After a brief pause, Caleb asked leading questions to get Yael to share stories of what happened after she left for Rome. As she spoke, her friends were equally riveted to every word she shared.

She worked at one of the palaces of Caesar's family. At first, she worked in the gardens, tending herbs and weeding the vegetables used in the royal kitchens. However, one afternoon as she waited in the kitchen for dinner to start, she was sexually assaulted by one of the Caesar men drunk with wine. She was unwilling to share any details of the events, but it made everyone who listened grieve, especially Yael's friends. Each of the girls embraced either Yael or her new friend, as they sought refuge from the words they were hearing.

Caleb helped pull from Yael to tell more of her story, but she always stopped before she could describe any of the mechanical aspects of her trauma. She shielded her father and friends from these horrors, seeing no good that would come from retelling the details of a story that ended with great sorrow. Caleb knew what this feeling was like, as had been in her place when he retold tales of killing either the Roman soldiers or the men on the boat. He had to stop when he talked about how he would aim his arrows when he launched them. He targeted the glutes of the rapist, knowing that it would prevent him from doing what he intended. He shot into the core of the man armed with a sword, knowing it would prevent him from running and swinging with full force. He hit the upper leg of the mobile archer, knowing it would impede his ability to aim and move. He was skilled at hurting people. He thought it shameful beyond words that this was his skill. He did know what good he could do with it.

Yael continued after a pause to wipe her face. She had obviously expressed some of the darker parts of her stay. She finished her tale as she described life after she was traded to the emperor at the end of an orgy one evening. Most importantly, all of the sexual assaults ended once she entered the House of Flavian. Despite the emperor's perversions towards women, he never assaulted her during the nearly one year he spent with her. She thought it was because she was a Hebrew. She served him and his house, and she was the maid of his concubine for nearly all of that time. Titus went so far as to honor her requests to be excluded from the rooms where orgies occurred. However, he did copulate with other women while his Hebrew concubine was in the room with him, and that made both of the girls grieve. When she met Eliza and Caleb, she was on lease to the Colosseum management as a box seat assistant, helping the wealthy guests with any requests that they had. She hated everything about the pits, and she was grateful that she never had to return.

Zev needed time to grieve after hearing this and add to his apologies. When they had arrived earlier, Zev was about to embark on another afternoon of drinking away his sorrows, and he was experiencing self-hatred the moment that Yael came.

Eliza's role was critical. She continually held Yael, touching her hair and holding her hand. From an outsider's perspective, the two of them were acting like any Hebrew sisters might. She had seen her aunt boldly speak to Hebrew men many times, even though this was a forbidden act in Hebrew culture, especially in public. Caleb had seen her do with the emperor, as well. She initiated a dialog with him, telling Zev how Yael had helped them meet the emperor, and she took off her ring and handed it to him to inspect. She had never let anyone hold her ring before that moment, including Caleb, and he was just as riveted to the details of her story as Zev and Yael's friends were.

While the man looked at the ring and shook his head, Eliza told him the details of how she and Yael had met, and she truthfully revealed Yael's role from the box seats to the pits and the palace. She followed Caleb's lead to make this moment about healing.

"Without your daughter's willingness to be in my life, I would never have been given this gift. Without her, I would never have had the courage to speak to the emperor. I am sure that without her, I, too, would have been sexually assaulted. Your beautiful daughter is dearer to me than my words can tell you. I speak the truth: she could make a claim on this ring as partly hers, and I would not dispute it," she said. When Zev handed it back to her, the awe on his face was replaced with more tears as Eliza slid it on one of Yael's fingers for her to experience and appreciate. Her friends covered their faces as if they had seen a ghost. Caleb knew that this was a cue from his cousin. Caleb put his arm on Zev and made him look at his eyes. Caleb exercised the power that the moment gave him once more.

"You must pause and understand that the wearer of this ring is perhaps the most powerful Hebrew alive today in all the Roman Empire. Eliza openly shares that ring with your daughter whom *you* sold into slavery!" Zev bowed his head, and Caleb waited for a few more tears to flow. However, Caleb's role as a healer was now more important than ever.

"My cousin loves your daughter enough to extend her this gift. She has brought both of us joy and stability. I think your daughter's life parallels that of our ancient grandfather Joseph and his time in Egypt with Pharaoh. Yahweh Himself has been with your daughter. I am sure this is true."

Everyone nodded and smiled. No one had thought about that until now.

Eliza placed the fingers of her hands in between Yael's, preventing her from taking the ring off and returning it. Yael's resistance eventually waned, and Eliza let go of her hands. Yael did not attempt to remove the ring. Caleb continued his display of power as a healer.

"I tell you the truth: you are looking at how Yeshua's promises are kept when He says that He can use all things for His glory. Your daughter helped us in a way that we cannot repay. All the while, she thinks she owes us for paying back the ransom required to free her from the slavery that you put her under. I say to you with certainty. All of us here are equals, Uncle."

Caleb abruptly stood up, and he extended his hand to Eliza to help her up as well. He asked everyone's understanding that he wished a few moments with Eliza alone. No one said anything. Zev was now broken down, and all the words that were shared this afternoon needed time to work. Zev needed time with his prodigal daughter, now that he had a new understanding not only of what she had done but who she was.

Caleb took Eliza a bit further out of the village and told her some of Uncle Rufus's story about how he learned that tactic. Eliza listened for several moments without asking any questions. After a long pause, she spoke.

"That man must come with us to the House of Healing. I am sure of it," Eliza said.

"I have already thought about that. Since I have walked away from him, my authority that came from my act will have waned, and I cannot make him join us. However, I can invite him, together with you and Yael."

"I like that idea," she said and then continued, "Caleb, you are a leader of our people. What you just did back there changed all of us, even those other girls. Uncle Rufus taught you well when he said that self-control and healing words are the greater power when compared to swords and dominance. I am in awe of what you just did. Total awe, my cousin," she said, reaching forward and embracing him in a bear hug.

That moment was most awkward for both of them. Eliza knew that Caleb required affirmation, and she felt a pang of guilt that she had not adequately provided that for him. But she also feared his response to her transparency. She felt fragile, sharing with him that he was a hero. She hated it when he called her stupid, even though she always played it down. However, his need to feel that he was the lion in the relationship was non-negotiable. By offering him the affirmation he needed, she was also a great winner. The Hebrew nation was a great winner.

When they returned to the village, Caleb stood at a distance as Eliza approached Yael. Yael stood up and enthusiastically introduced her to her childhood friends as her long-lost sister, making all of them giggle. They all greeted each other the way Hebrew schoolgirls do, and one of them took all the girls to her house to finish preparing the village meal. They needed to cook the vegetables, grind salt, and set candles. They all ran off without looking back at Caleb. He now understood why his uncle had warned him of the power and its impact. Absolute authority, when exercised, removes intimacy. It fuels our addictive tendencies. It creates holes in our psyche as we lose others who no longer feel safe loving us unconditionally. In that moment, Caleb was lonely unlike any time in his life, and the only tools at his disposal in his heart were prayer and the desire to flee from sin.

Yet, the act of dominating another man was worth the temporary separation it caused. Yael's honor had been restored in her hometown. He paused with his hands on his hips to enjoy the moment. He glanced at the village and saw that Zev endured where Caleb and Eliza left him and stared at Caleb. He obviously remained intimidated of him, and Uncle Rufus told him that any future relationship with this person would be unpredictable. The moment was equally awkward for Caleb. The only two girls he knew in this village were gone, and he was not invited to join them. At this time of day, he could not use hunting as an escape to leave. He just stood there. Eventually, one of the women brought him water to drink and bathe with, pointing out to him where dinner would be served and that he should go there. She waited for him to finish washing before reiterating where they would be as she left to go back to her home.

As expected, everyone showed up for free meat. Caleb ate his meal with the other boys, who asked him lots of questions about hunting, and he told them of the deer he shot a few weeks earlier. Some of the older men also sat with boys and listened, as well, as they had not been told any new stories recently. Caleb complemented the older men who prepared the meat, and he had no less than four servings of the venison. Everyone in the village ate their fill that night, and there were nearly no leftovers.

When dinner was over, Caleb stood and walked towards the girls. The protocols of Hebrew culture took over, and the only ones who spoke to him were members of his biological family. Eliza introduced him to everyone. However, it was obvious that Eliza and Yael had been talking about him.

Although no one said anything, they all looked at him. Caleb had one thing left to do.

"Yael, can I talk to you?" he said. She stood up and glanced back at her friends, then walked towards Caleb. They all whispered.

"Please excuse us," he said. Keeping with Hebrew custom, they only walked a few steps away so as not to be heard, but he dared not take her out of anyone's sight, as that was a sinful and potentially considered an adulterous act. Nonetheless, he reached out and took her hand. She accepted, despite both of them knowing that this was inappropriate behavior for the unmarried.

"I am sorry for that event, I was about—" but she cut him off.

"No, Caleb, stop. Please let me thank you for protecting my honor. That act you did back there changed all of us. When I saw you throw your sword to the ground and treat my father as honorably as you did, I was speechless. I was grateful."

Yael looked to the ground, reached out, and took his other hand before return her gaze to his.

"You are right. He did not deserve your grace. But I think you really helped him when you did that. You know what? I thought I had seen a boy becoming a man in the Colosseum. I was blind. I was watching a young man become a great man. It is my turn to be truthful. You are the one that saved Eliza and me."

She maintained eye contact while she spoke, and all of her childhood friends stared at them, both motionless and speechless.

Caleb knew the moment to be tender, but he was not ready for it. However, his attraction to her was undeniable. He released their handhold and pointed back to her friends.

As they returned, Yael took off the ring and gave it back to Eliza. This time, she took it back as she made eye contact with each of them. The girls stood up and grabbed Yael by her cloak, pulling her away as all six of them ran around the corner to stop and talk. Their high-pitched giggling made Caleb smile.

He heard all the girls laughing, and he knew that both Yael and Eliza needed to. He had seen them crying on the boat ride home too many times.

That moment with Yael had been too intimate. Her father walked up to Caleb when he was not looking and spoke to him.

"What is your intention with my daughter?" Zev asked.

Caleb looked at the man and thought, *Who are you to ask questions about loyalty and integrity, old man? My intentions are none of your business! That is something I would only talk about with her father, and you have not earned that title!*

But he did not speak those words; instead, he took a deep breath and said, "Uncle, I am not sure I know. She is dear both to Eliza and me. I think you know that, now," he said.

The man nodded and walked away. Caleb decided to walk towards Eliza and the girls, and he found them passing around Eliza's ring and trying it on. They were laughing uncontrollably but stopped as he approached. Eliza spoke up first.

"I like this place," she said. Caleb smiled and nodded back.

As the evening's social events ended, many people came up to Caleb and thanked him for his gift of meat, and many offered him a few copper coins for his efforts to feed a village struggling to survive. He took all their coin, immediately giving to Eliza for management. They all returned to Yael's childhood home to sleep. There was no conversation about tomorrow. Caleb slept in the room with Yael's father. Yael and Eliza slept together. Emotional fatigue set in, and all four of them were asleep quickly.

LEAVING GEZER

Everyone woke up before sunrise, and Yael immediately tried to return to her role as oldest daughter and begin the first meal preparations. Quickly, she was upset at the lack of staples. They were nearly out of olive oil, and the only flour that they had was rancid. She complained to Eliza the whole time, and Eliza sent Caleb to the cart to get some of the staples that she had purchased in Joppa. While breakfast was cooked, Caleb left with his bow, telling everyone he was going to a nearby ravine to look for tracks and that he would be back mid-morning. He took a couple of steps outside and realized that he did not want to be alone. He went back inside to sit with the girls.

"Back so fast?" Eliza asked.

"I would rather not be alone right now," he said. He set his bow down and poured himself another cup of tea before standing next to where the girls were preparing the rest of the meal. Yael looked at him and spoke thoughtfully.

"Caleb, I was so scared you were going to kill my father. I did not know your uncle taught you to do that," Yael said. Caleb told her about how his uncle taught him to intimidate when he had the upper hand, not only to prevent future occurrences but to make right the wrongs in progress. He apologized to her for scaring her, but not for what he did.

Eliza had a flashback that she could not keep to herself as she stared at the two of them from the other side of the kitchen.

"You two look just like my aunt and uncle right now. In the mornings in Tamar, Auntie would cook food in the kitchen, all the while talking with my uncle, and my uncle would watch her work. That was the only time each day that two of them had to stay connected, as the evenings almost always meant visitors. You two just look and act the same," she said. They both looked at her like she was from another tribe.

Zev walked in, and Yael got up to greet him, kissing him on the cheek as is Hebrew custom. Eliza stood up to do the same, but he raised a hand to stop her.

"You are not my daughter. I cannot accept this honor from you," he said, still feeling the wounds from last night.

She leaned forward and kissed him nonetheless.

"I honor the father of my sister," she said, standing next to Yael as she heated a pan to cook bread. She had never had a sister, and it was not until that moment that she realized that she had always wanted one. Her mother's sister was the most influential person in her life, and her loss seemed more impactful in this moment. The rabbi told her that waves of sorrow would overcome her at unanticipated times, and she knew that this was one such moment. She never saw it coming, though.

For his part, Zev was able to respond and help her when he saw her tears.

"Your true father may not be with you now, but I am sure that he loved you a lot and has lifted you up in his prayers, wherever he may be. For what you offered my daughter, I can think of you as family," he said. Eliza could not speak any words of gratitude as the pain of her aunt's memories had not yet subsided.

"I tell you the truth. I have never had such an event as we have had this last day in my home. My daughter returns, and I behave poorly. I am rightfully reprimanded for my actions and now receive blessings from the children who reprimanded me. Two young people of great authority enter into my daughter's life and place her at their level, even while she is in slavery, a result of a crime that I committed. Surely, this is a world of folly and amazement," he says.

"From the rabbi who reprimanded you. That is what you meant, right?" added Yael.

"Rabbi? What do you mean?" he asked.

With that, Yael told her father the story of their time in the palace that was not disclosed last night. She gave him the version that did not include any reference to the orgy that was about to happen. She said that all three of them had been invited to the royal palace in the Palatine Hill of Rome immediately after Caleb had fought and won in the Colosseum. The emperor came to them after they finished getting ready for evening festivities, and Eliza engaged him in conversation that lasted much of the night. The following morning, he asked Eliza to stay and become his spiritual teacher, and he asked her what he should call her. The answer was "rabbi."

"I am not a rabbi!" said Eliza. However, secretly she had been considering the idea.

"Wasn't there another female rabbi?" Zev said.

"That was my mother," said Caleb.

"She was my aunt," added Eliza.

"Father, I should have told you that. Remember the—" Yael started to speak, but Zev interrupted.

"You are not only the family of a royal household but also of the husband-and-wife Hebrew scholars? What else are you going to tell me?" he asked.

"Well, my dad was a scholar, that is for sure. My mom was a great teacher, so if that makes her a scholar, then the answer to your question is yes," Caleb said.

Caleb knew his role; Yael had reiterated it to him yesterday. He was their leader. He was also their healer. After a few more questions, Caleb hijacked the conversation and decided it was time to ask a more important question. This one was not about the past. It was about the present.

"Uncle, the three of us, children, are wounded people. As you heard some of our stories last night, we witnessed and participated in evil events, and our souls are hurt. We observed atrocities that should happen only in the pits of hell, and we need help if we are to heal. We are leaving this day to travel to Kedron to visit the House of Healing. The rabbis there are adept and helping people who have suffered what we have, and they know how to help us be restored. Eliza and I went to them before, and they helped us greatly. We all, well, Eliza and I have talked, and we think that you should come with us. You experienced great loss and need help, too. Will you come with us?"

Yael was frightened. She had not mentioned any of this to her father, and she feared his disapproval. She stared at his face as Caleb confronted him.

Zev shook his head as if to say "no," but instead, he said, "Yes."

"I am weary of seeking. I am weary of seeking wealth. I am weary of seeking a wife. I am weary of seeking everything. If these rabbis are as good as you say, then let us go."

They ate breakfast without speaking on grave topics anymore. Zev complimented their cooking, and Caleb

Of Healing and Finding Home

observed how kind and sincere words put a smile on Yael's face. Afterward, Eliza and Yael braided each other's hair while Caleb walked with Zev as he made rounds in the village, letting leadership know that he was leaving for Kedron with the kids and would be gone a couple of days. Out of respect, Caleb said nothing as they walked to the two houses. However, he was fascinated at how Zev introduced him differently to the two different people he needed to visit. The first time, when they met the mayor, Zev's voice was fast and shaky.

"This is Caleb from last night. He and his cousin helped my daughter get out of Rome early, and they did some stuff together and are now, well, close, and they want me to go with them to a place to heal with some rabbis. His parents were rabbis, actually. I will be gone for a few days. Can you watch my home while I am away?"

From there, they traveled to the irrigation manager's house. He said, "this is the boy from last night who shook me up and got us the meat. He and my daughter and her sister, or his cousin… It's complicated, you know. Anyway, they convinced me to go with them to see a house in Kedron. We are going today, so while I am gone, can you give my assignments to someone else?"

As they walked back, Zev confided in Caleb. "You can see that you make me nervous," he said. Caleb picked this moment to be a bit more tender.

"I did not plan to do that to you yesterday. My uncle was a legate, and he trained me in Roman tactics. I saw you as a threat to Yael, and I took ownership of defending her, and that was the best idea I had. As you can see, when I am with my girls, I am protective of them," he said. His uncle told him that he could never apologize, even if he felt that he must. It would ruin future use of this power with others, and he would second guess himself the next time he needed to exercise absolute dominance. "They are dear to me, both of them," he ended.

"Well, you made your point. You treated my daughter better than I did. I remain ashamed of that," he said. They walked the rest of the way back to Zev's home without speaking.

The wagon was fully loaded, and both the girls were wearing their thicker Roman cloaks, as it felt like a thick cloak kind of day. They began their journey with both the girls riding in the cart and the boy and the man walking. They stopped mid-morning for a break, and Caleb began telling Zev the story that started when they returned to Tamar from their night in Kedron. Zev listened but used a lot of body language to express his feelings as he shared. Zev was a conservative Hebrew man, and he could not understand how Eliza was allowed to travel across occupied territory alone. He could not understand how two Hebrew spiritual leaders would allow two cousins not yet completing their *bar* or *bat mitzvah*[1] to travel to a foreign city in Philistia alone. The stories of the boat ride and the boat wreck were riveting, but even more interesting to Zev was how quickly Eliza forgave Balbi. Yael was equally amazed that Caleb was able to listen to Eliza and not kill Balbi when he had the chance. She had never heard that story. When they shared how Balbi became a Yeshua follower and Caleb released him from slavery with no consequence, Yael stood with her mouth open. For his part, Zev said many praises to Yahweh but had nothing to add.

Caleb could tell that Zev was not a fighting man but only a hard-working man, so he left out many of the details of combat. None of them had heard the story of Ronan, the man who Caleb competed with in the gladiator pits, and he took out the note that had his home village name and his parents' name. Eliza reached over and held her cousin's forearm when he spoke of Ronan, not realizing that he had carried the burden of another man's death for weeks without disclosing it.

"You are truly a good man," said Zev, as parts of Caleb's character were now overpowering the young man he met the night before. When Caleb said that he was going to return there one day, no one spoke. However, he did take that moment to look at Yael and smile; there was obviously another adventure to be had.

They all told of their time in the Colosseum, but it was apparent that no amount of description could relay the ambiance of the organized killing that happened there. They all repeated to Zev that what they saw was horrible, and they never want to return.

Soon, they were underway, and the roads were smooth and unoccupied by Roman troops. They made great progress, and they reached their first-night destination city without any events. Checking into the inn was most challenging for them as a Hebrew lot. Eliza was paying for everyone, but Zev was the oldest male and was responsible for everyone. He was also ashamed that he could not pay. Caleb intervened.

"We invited you to join us, and we are responsible for all of this expense, Uncle. You will room with me, and the girls will have their own room," he said. Zev nodded, and his sense of shame made Yael feel shame, too. Eliza held her close, and the moment passed.

THE WAGONS OF SLAVERY

When Matthew asked the wagon driver where they were going, the slave did not answer. The soldier riding on horseback next to them spoke instead, demonstrating why the Romans were masters at group submission.

"If you ask that question again, I will cut out both your tongue and the ear of the one you speak to," he said, without ever making eye contact. For effect, he unsheathed his gladius as he spoke, holding it above shoulder height pointing upwards. The only way it could now travel was down, and that meant down on a Jew who had no way to defend himself from a razor-sharp blade bearing the weight of a trained military man. Something would get cut off if Matthew responded any way other than in an affirmation. The act of removing a body part demonstrated no fear of intervention, and it took them nearly no time to complete. There was no trial nor extensive preparation needed. And the act was always watched by everyone, making its impact great. All that was left was to execute the act. Every soldier who was in leadership was trained to follow through on their threats. As such, they were never made lightheartedly.

To ensure that the point was made, another soldier moved his horse so as to be right next to where Matthew sat in case he needed to act. He also unsheathed his blade and held it over his head. All the women and most of the men on the cart covered their heads, and Matthew was no exception. Matthew was no fighter. Matthew had also seen Jews killed by Roman soldiers and knew it was not above them to kill them all.

As instructed, the Jews in the cart complied, asking no more questions of either the driver or the soldiers. The desire to find answers to their questions was squelched by the fear of what might happen if they try. After the horses moved away and the weapons were put back in their sheaths, the parents of the students talked only amongst themselves for the rest of the day.

For their part, the Romans followed protocol for slave transport. They camped next to a river: this allowed them to position the Jews where they could have ample access to drinking water and resources to wash and bathe as well as cut off a known pathway to escape. Crossing a river in a desert leaves marks on the other side that cannot be avoided. Crossing the river was not an option, and even the dumbest of Jews knew this.

In the morning, both Katya and Matthew were groggy from a poor night's sleep without any protection from the cold other than what they were wearing when they entered the village. They boarded the wagon at sunrise, but the soldiers did not speak to them, as was their tradition, until they had been traveling long enough for the sun to be up in the sky. They would stop them in a conspicuous place where any attempt to escape could readily be tracked and feed them. Oddly enough, no one in their group tried to run away, thinking that a cart of twenty could easily outmaneuver or outrun only three soldiers. Normally, day one of slavery included casualties. That did not happen that day. This group was either wise or lacked the courage to try.

Of Healing and Finding Home

At mid-day on the second day, they were within visual sight of Jerusalem. The cart veered to the north and stopped within a stone's throw of a walled but small city next to Jerusalem. Outside the city walls were a series of perhaps a hundred tents, lined up in rows, with latrines at the end of each row.

"Welcome to Tent City. This will be your new home now," the soldiers said without dismounting from horseback. The three of them turned and began walking towards the city's walled gates. When they were out of range of hearing, Katya spoke to Matthew.

"I think that city is where Yael went after she was raped, you know, when she met the old woman?" Katya asked. Matthew had never seen her so timid, but she had also never been a captive of the Roman military establishment. She had never been to Jerusalem and only had Yael's stories to construct a visual equivalency of the stories Yael told her.

Katya still remembered the day that Yael told her about the raping. The two sisters both had their babies and were together for Caleb's *brit milah*, circumcision ceremony. She remembered the power her sister displayed as she stepped behind the altar at the temple with her newborn. Only rabbis were allowed behind the altar, and it was not yet public knowledge that Yael had been given the title of the rabbi by Luke. Some wished to speak up and say something to stop what they perceived as blasphemy, but she kept calm and spoke with authority before they could organize their words.

"Today, my husband and our rabbi Mishi will be our *mohel*[2] *and perform the act of removing the foreskin of the penis for our son, Caleb, as Yahweh has instructed him to do. This is our faith's unique act, required by Yahweh of old to be considered among the community of His chosen people. It is also required by the Pharisees of all Hebrew men who have descended from* the twelve tribes. It is a mark of the covenant between Jehovah and Abraham. And, for this, we will follow our people and our faith," she said.

"However, our Yeshua taught us through his servant Paul a different message of greater worth. Paul asks us some questions. Hear them and listen," she said, holding her head up and making eye contact with many people, as the altar in Correae was above where everyone stood and watched the power in which she taught Yeshua's words for the remainder of the ceremony.

"Was anyone called while circumcised? Let him not be circumcised. Circumcision is nothing, and uncircumcision is nothing,"[3] she said. She paused and made eye contact with as many as she could, both male and female, all while rocking her baby.

"Even more important than the words that Paul shared was this evidence: Yeshua came for all of us, not just the Jews who have a history of circumcision. Do not let this ceremony convince you that we are Jews or are followers of Yeshua. This ceremony is a gift from our pre-Messiah past, not a requirement of the new faith with Yeshua that the Messiah spoke of in the writings of Isaiah and other prophets," she said, handing the baby to its father.

"Lastly, as many of you have heard, I was raped by a Roman man, and this child is the result of that crime. It is not my husband's child, but he now comes before you not just to be the mohel of this child but to publicly proclaim that in the same sense that Yeshua adopts all who want eternal life, my husband adopts this child, following the example set before him by Yeshua's mother and father here on the earth!"

She needed a moment to breathe, and Mishi stepped next to her, placing the items of the brit milah on the altar, blessing them with the ancient chants from the sacred scrolls that he had memorized as a boy. When it was done, he turned to the crowd in attendance and continued with his wife's remarks.

"I did not ask her to say these things," he said, getting a small chuckle from the crowd but also validating her point. "This child is biologically a gentile, yet I bring him before the altar to experience brit milah, completing the union of gentile and Jew in the life of this precious babe that only Yahweh could have ordained. Let no man, and let no woman deny a child because of who he is or what he stands for. This is the Lord's child, just like me. Just like you. I tell you the truth. I take him as my own with pride and joy that words cannot describe."

He completed the cut, and as the baby cried, Mishi attached the boy's first *yarmulke*[4] *to his head, signifying his status as a Jew, and they paraded him around the village while everyone cheered on in acceptance.*

ELIZA IN TRANSITION

Eliza was a fragile girl, capable of emotional breakdowns and feeling paralyzed when action was required. In the last few months, she had been held down as she was about to be raped. She had survived a shipwreck and felt paralyzed on the deck of the sinking ship even after Caleb had jumped into the water and started swimming to the shore. She fell apart on the docks once she learned that her duffel bag of Egyptian towels had been stolen. She was nearly fourteen years old, and when those damaged parts of her personality came up, they were on display in a way that left Caleb feeling embarrassed. That moment at the docks when she found out that her precious towels were gone was one of those moments of embarrassment that Caleb would prefer to forget.

Then, there was the Eliza that would appear in history books. There was the young girl who showed no fear telling the story of the Messiah to the emperor, calling for him to be baptized. There was Eliza, the teenaged "rabbi" and member of the House of Flavian, with unlimited freedom and power to command any part of the Roman military. Yet, even with this power, she displayed a seemingly limitless capacity to pardon nearly any crime done against her. For all practical purposes, she was both the freest and most forgiving Jew in the world.

Only Yael was there when she talked to the emperor. Even the slaves that served him were absent.

"Emperor Titus, your brother Rufus told my cousin and me stories about you when he would stay with us. He told us of all of your physical competitions and your great campaigns all around the world. He said that the two of you had already lived ten lifetimes of experiences together before you were thirty years old," she said, looking him directly in the eye after asking him to sit down with her in a moment when she knew he intended to rape her. She saw the emperor perplexed by her line of stories; he was used to women attempting to get him to stop his intended violation of their bodies, but he was not used to personal stories.

"You know, Rufus told us that he thought you would become emperor one day, and he had no concern for the fate of the Roman Empire under your leadership," she said. She shifted her position, rearranging her revealing clothing to maintain a sense of modesty.

"But you know what he also said? He said that no matter what you two achieved, the rewards never really satisfied you. Uncle Rufus collected many items of great worth, but he gave them all away. He had unlimited access to gold and silver, the spoils of your combined efforts. Isn't that true?" she asked. And with great courage, she stared at the ruler of the Roman Empire in the eyes and waited for an answer. Seldom did people live when they asked a probing question of the emperor unless they were citizens and members of the Senate.

The emperor nodded.

"You love female flesh, and you desire mine, yes? You know that I am a young virgin, and this is of interest to you, and you know my cousin will kill to protect me, yes?" she said. Her Greek was flawless, and her use of the pronoun you and its forms was perfect. She made him think.

"I am listening," he said, leaning back and putting his hands on the ground behind him as he sat in a cross-legged position.

"I know the freedom and the joy you seek. It is the same one that Caleb seeks. Just like you, we are seekers of the truth and seekers of happiness. It is the same truth that your brother Rufus sought. We do not want to be victims of our addictions and desires. We want to control them. Even now, you struggle with your desire to take me. There is little I can do to stop you, but I do not fear that you will do anything evil to me. You are the emperor, but something seems wrong to you, and you need help seeing why you feel this, don't you?" she said, exercising even more courage. All the while, the emperor continued to nod his head in agreement.

Throughout, Yael stood in the distance, watching her new sister speak into the heart of the leader of the world. She was carving away the decoration that surrounded his soul, and he was letting her. For reasons that none will ever know, he trusted her.

"Yeshua came into this world to free us from our addictions, our pains, and our desires to hurt others. He teaches us how to do this by trusting His Word. Would you like to hear some of His Word? I wrote many of them down on paper many years ago, and there are copies of His Word all over your empire. Indeed, there are perhaps a hundred copies in this very city. Many of your prison guards have heard these words, and they come to our synagogues to learn the meaning of them. If you like, I will not only tell you the words that Yeshua used, but I will tell you what they mean. Your brother said these words created the most change-invoking experience of his life," she said, turning her head to one side and staring at the man as if he were still a teenage boy asking the question, "What shall I do with my life?"

"Rufus told me only pieces of what he heard, and I admit, I did not understand what he said. I did see how much they meant to him. If you know Rufus, and you know these words and their meaning, I will listen," Titus said.

With her greatest act of courage yet, she broke eye contact with Titus and looked at Yael.

"Come, sit with the little emperor, and listen to the words from the living Yahweh."

Yael made eye contact with the emperor, and he acknowledged her. Eliza spoke of the emperor of the Roman Empire using a diminutive language, in the same way she would speak to a student, but she did so with a tone of affection. Yael was nervous when she sat next to the emperor. After all, she had been there when this man had raped women, and she was scared of him.

Eliza talked well into the night. Titus heard her tell the story of the birth of Yeshua and how it was foretold literally thousands of years before. She told him of John the Baptist, and she sang Zechariah's song to Titus. She told him of the lineage of Yeshua and his tests in the wilderness. The emperor was most interested in those tests, and he asked many questions.

And she spoke of all of his healings. After all, her aunt's teacher was the healer Luke. Of course, she knew the most about this topic.

Once she began telling him of the many parables of Jesus, Titus had heard enough. Something had come over him, and he no longer needed to listen.

"Of my own volition and my own best efforts, I do not allow myself the life satisfaction that you obviously have. I could have long since taken your body, but you need not

Of Healing and Finding Home

be afraid. Nor do you have anger or show any signs of seeking something from me that you have not already asked for. Truly this message is a gift, is it not? What must I do to receive this gift?" he asked.

"I will teach you a prayer, and you must say it. You say it to Yeshua, not to me. Also, you must also be baptized. Both are a part of our faith. Both are public professions, so you cannot do these things behind the walls of your palace," she said.

Eliza took a piece of parchment and a pen and rapidly composed a note. She folded it and gave it to Yael.

"Yael, can you take a message to your rabbi in your synagogue and have him make ready to baptize the emperor as soon as possible?" she asked. For her part, Yael froze. Eliza repeated herself, and Yael snapped out of her trance.

"Yeah, right. I will go right now," she said, and when she stood up, she was still unable to express the breadth of the feelings she had after watching a man she thought to be despicable accept the reality of the Messiah. She took two steps towards the entryway and turned around like a teenage girl might.

"But I need to change out of these clothes before I go running on the streets of Rome in the middle of the night," and with that, all three of them laughed loudly.

CLOSE TO JERUSALEM

Matthew stood up and took his first steps while chained to all the other men. Walking the short distance from the cart to the staging area would be slow. Out from the larger canvas tent in Tent City walked a soldier clad in a dark red cloak. He wore a large but only partial helmet that made him appear much taller than he actually was. Both Katya and Matthew had heard a description of Roman administrators and their garb, but neither had ever seen one. They speculated to themselves that this man must be theirs.

"Welcome to the New Jerusalem," he said in perfect Hebrew.

"Each of you will work here and shall be accounting for your time and efforts. We will judge if you have done what we asked," he said. For the next moments, he explained their process at this labor camp and recorded their information on a parchment. He showed each of them a thick piece of papyrus, telling them he would make one for each of them that evening, and they needed to get theirs in the morning, once he had all of their names and home villages.

"You will show us this card any time we ask for it. The penalty for not having this card is death. You will each eat two meals a day, and this card will be necessary to get your portion of food in the morning, then you shall go to work. You will have a mark placed on it each day by your foreman at the end of your shift. If you do not have the day's mark on your card, you will not be served any food that evening. Too many of you do not work hard enough during the day to earn dinner."

He gestured for four of the guards to begin traveling to each person, removing their chains and replacing each one of them with a single iron band on their left foot. The very first person in line objected, and the administrator pointed at one of the armed soldiers. The soldier came over and attempted to strike the man with the flat side of his sword on the top of his shoulder. The man raised his arm to protect himself, and the soldier rotated his blade, so the edge came down first. It hit the man's outstretched hand and passed through it. The blade stopped moving when it came to a stop on his shoulder blade.

"Do not resist our banding of you. It will cause you pain that you can avoid," said the administrator in a calm voice.

The band signified that they were temporary slaves. Had they been permanent slaves, they would have been branded on their forearms. Temporary slavery meant that it would end, and that gave Katya and Matthew hope.

Once the last of them were banded, the administrator continued.

"That is good. Lastly, you will be allowed to leave and return home, but only when I say you can—this camp is not a death sentence to people who do what is asked of them. You are serving the empire by working here. Once you leave, you will receive a new card to possess that will exempt you from taxation for a period of one year, in exchange for your service in this place," he shared.

Administrators all had individual choices as to how they wanted to govern their slaves/interns. Some govern with an iron rod, using corporal punishment as the primary instructional tool. Others rule with hope and positive affirmation. When all the administration heads would gather to discuss their strategies, there was a heated debate as to which one was the most effective in helping them reach their quotas and achieve bonuses. It was not yet obvious which strategy this administrator valued more.

Katya did not think like that. She had a great desire to follow the rules and avoid conflict. She was most scared that he was not telling them the truth and would harm them all at the first opportunity. She immediately wondered how long they would be in this internment camp. She wondered if she was soon to be raped like her little sister. Above all, she wondered what was happening with her daughter. No one here would know.

The administrator continued his introductions.

"The only exceptions to this rule are for those who ask if they can leave their term of service early. If you ask, you will regret it, the Roman way," he said, gesturing to the killing fields, covered in crucifixes awaiting use.

Matthew had heard many stories of Jews who had worked in these temporary camps, as many of them had traveled to Correae afterward, seeking a form of asylum and rest. He immediately began positive self-talk that he could endure this if he followed the rules. He knew that he and Katya would not live out the rest of their days in this place. They would be here only for a time. They would leave with an exemption from taxation for a year, and he knew exactly how he would use this exemption. The village had been accumulating a larger-than-normal stash of gold to purchase many Roman bricks to increase the quality of the roads into and out of Correae. Normally, the purchase of so many bricks would be a taxable event. With this card, he would be exempt from those taxes: all he needed to do was show evidence that he used his wealth and not the village's wealth to build the road. His mind was already scheming.

The administrator then placed a wooden chair and a desk in front of where he stood, gesturing for the first person to come to him.

After a series of people, he called up Matthew. "What is it that you do back home?" he asked. There was no way that Matthew would tell him that he screened people as they came to settle into their village to see if they could be trusted with the village secret of a gold mine.

"I am a farmer, and we have beasts of burden," he said. Two answers were what they wanted to hear to offer some variety with their placement.

"Very well. You will be sold," he said.

That was the last thing Matthew wanted. He knew his wife needed him, and he was not going to allow them to separate her.

"I am also a builder in our village. I can carry baskets of rock," he said. This was truthful but not complete. He carried baskets of gold ore to their smelter, but he was no builder of houses other than the one he made with his father-in-law fifteen years ago.

"Very well. Report to the city walls each day," said the administrator.

Katya was asked the same question; regardless of their answer, all the women were assigned to the company kitchen. There were only six women who made the trip to Tamar to drop off their children; all the other escorts were males. The Romans needed help in the kitchen, no matter what her other skills might be.

HOUSE OF HEALING REVISITED

"Come, let's continue onto the House of Healing. We should reach it at the end of the day," said Eliza as they stood up after their morning meal at the inn.

"Very well, the rabbi has spoken," said Caleb most playfully. Anytime Eliza put on her bossy attitude, Caleb found pleasure in toning it down using formal language. Zev only shook his head and smirked as these children continued their transition to adults. It still seemed preposterous that this young girl could explain some of the mysteries of the Messiah to the emperor and be called a rabbi, only to find herself sitting in a cart and getting picked on by her teenage cousin.

As they rode in the cart, the two girls took turns braiding each other's hair while the men walked behind. It was common for Hebrew women to let their hair down at night and braid it in the morning. The two girls were both proficient at caring for the other's hair after many weeks of doing this. Normally, this was done away from men so as to not completely expose their heads to them. This created an undue risk of exposure that the culture deemed preventable, and each of the tribes had adopted it as a cultural policy when in the presence of non-family. However, with Caleb and Zev being family by all metrics, the girls did not care. The cart owner was a hired hand, so none of them were concerned with his opinion of their behavior.

With their cart full of fresh bread, hummus, and fruit, they set off for Kedron. The temperatures were much warmer than yesterday, and none of them needed their warmer cloaks. Yael and Eliza agreed that they would be reaching Kedron with plenty of time to spare, and they would go to the market and replace everyone's soiled clothing. This would require some extra time in the afternoon, as they needed to be tailored to fit them perfectly. Everyone in their group except Caleb needed new apparel. Zev's clothing was the most tattered and dirty, but his pride prevented traditional appreciation gestures, as he was not used to accepting gifts from children that were not his own. As such, he promised to pay Eliza back, not knowing she carried the equivalent of the entire village's coins in her bag. Eliza spoke up and rebutted, thoughtfully choosing her words.

"Nonsense. Yael is my sister now, and that makes you my father. I believe we already agreed to this, yes?" she said. To cement her point, she approached him and kissed him on the cheek, as a good Hebrew daughter would. He bowed his head in acceptance, but in his heart, he did not yet accept her.

Once their clothing was complete, they headed in from the city's protective wall and towards the House of Healing. They arrived well before sunset when the evening events started. Neither Caleb nor Eliza realized how close they were to the city center, and they arrived quickly. Caleb and Eliza got out of the cart, thanking the driver for his service. They knew not how long they would be there in residence, but they experienced life here before, and they knew how things operated. Healing cannot be rushed. Before Caleb could finish the transaction, Eliza recognized their rabbi walking towards them. Caleb quickly finished paying him and ran to give the man a hug as well. Yael was right behind them.

"Rabbi Dor!" they said, as they embraced, each one closing their eyes while they let the man embrace them. As a leader in the faith, he embraced all Yeshua followers with the same level of endearment. He also hugged Zev and Yael, even though he did not know who they were.

The two cousins were children again, and they rapidly spoke to him about their journey. They interrupted each other, and everyone laughed repeatedly. They told of the trip across the sea and getting shipwrecked. They spoke of the prophecy given to them as well as the underground synagogues they found all over Rome. He asked few questions, but he did not need to, as the story of the last month of their life was not going to stop until they had finished it. All the while, the volunteers in residence unloaded the cart and moved the contents to two rooms on opposite ends of their facility. All the volunteers greeted them, bowing and offering any assistance that they needed. This place would be their home until the rabbis told them otherwise. There was currently no one else in residence, and the place was theirs.

Yael was briefly introduced, and she felt no hesitancy to join in their game. Yael told Rabbi Dor of Caleb's deeds in the Colosseum, and she added many of the details of the House of Caesar as they attempted to bribe him to become a gladiator for them.

"I have seen many evils originate from the House of Caesar, but never have I heard of any house offering half a talent of silver for each battle won in the Colosseum. Caleb could have been the richest and most powerful Jew in all of Rome, yet he gracefully declined. I tell you, a deed like this may never be seen again," she added. Caleb's ego filled with appreciation, but it quickly was turned into a bashful appreciation by some other negative and remarkable words from Eliza of the sort she liked to share to bring Caleb back down to earth. He hated it when she belittled him in public, and Yael had seen her do it a couple of times.

The storytelling continued until the sun was about to set. Although winter was coming to an end, the desert environment of Judah meant that temperatures at the end of the day dropped rapidly. Rabbi Dor asked them to come into the entry hall and sit by the large fire to stay warm. Both Eliza and Caleb had spent time in this place, telling stories of the hurt at the bottom of their souls. They took their seats, ignoring any responsibilities, and allowed themselves to rest. Volunteers brought them fresh bread and hot tea. They had no other destinations to reach. This was as far as their plan included.

Even before they reached the tales of the emperor's acceptance of Yeshua, Zev and the rabbis were in states of awe. Surviving a shipwreck, meeting the emperor, battling in the Colosseum, and being given a membership ring of the House of Flavian were the stories of plays enacted at the great amphitheaters of the world. They were unbelievable stories from honest teenaged Jews who had just lost their parents to the ravages of Roman occupation. Yet, a display of the ring, the signed decree with the emperor's seal on it, and a vast payment for Yael's early release from freedom proved otherwise.

Rabbi Dor did not wait to begin his craft. They were seekers, and they needed the truth.

"You three are courageous children. It is reasonable that there will be tales written of your adventures as well as songs to be sung. You all traveled to the heart of the empire and returned with the exact thing that you most wanted. You all sought freedom and an opportunity to help your families. It appears that you achieved your goals, have you not?"

He looked at each one, and he would not let them continue any conversation until they spoke their own words back to him, affirming what he said.

"Yes, I have a ring and a royal decree that will demand any Roman soldiers comply with my requests for information and freedom of my parents," said Eliza.

"I am a free woman, and I have two new family members who have replaced the ones that I have lost," said Yael, wiping away the tears as she spoke those words for the first time, "I am pleased beyond any words that I can share." She was already beginning to feel the freedom associated with residence in the House of Healing.

"I have again killed and again found it leaving me without peace. I have much to learn about how to use my bow and my sword, but I also watched the skills of a centurion begin the healing journey in my new family. Just like my uncle before me, I have found an identity protecting those that I love," said Caleb. Caleb's sense of freedom also reached a zenith, and he openly took Yael's hand, interlocking his fingers with hers, as he had seen his parents do. Yael did not look at her father but only accepted Caleb's gesture.

With that, Zev stepped up and began acting like a Hebrew patriarch. "These children did not deserve their traumatic experiences. Yet, they come back to us and heal us all with their actions. I tell you this: even while they were wounded, they were bringing about healing to others. I was too weak to see how wounded I was. I am most grateful to Caleb for breaking me of my blindness," he said. He addressed him in the diminutive, but it was with great endearment.

Yael looked at Caleb: the boy had earned her father's greatest acceptance. She placed her other hand on to of Caleb's and smiled.

"You are not married, nor have you entered into erusin. I call on both of you to avoid the sins of your mother and cease this behavior until you are husband and wife," spoke the rabbi.

"I am sorry," said Caleb as he let go of Yael's hand. He bowed his head in shame.

The wisdom of the rabbi emerged: "You both have lost family and seek to replace it with someone who honors you and loves you. You each seem to see these traits in each other. However, the truth of your circumstances is making you blind to the lessons learned from our past. Let us all spend time with you and help you see what has happened to your souls."

They nodded in agreement.

"Caleb, you have no family to guide you through the erusin process, so I will do that for you and with you. Do not touch this girl until you are ready to put a ring on her and build a life with her and share all you have with her. Do you understand me?" asked Dor.

"Yes, Rabbi Dor," he said, maintaining eye contact.

Caleb had not used terms of endearment with Yael, but with his actions, he had already made it known that he loved her. He now needed to act like a man and honor her with more than his bow and sword.

Zev sat in wonder as the rabbi's words began to refine Caleb's soul. For the first time, Zev saw Caleb as a young man who needed guidance and not as an intimidating soldier in training.

"Enough of this discipline! My friends, you are all greatly wounded. In the same way we must dig deep to scrape the dirt from a wound, we will need to dig and scrape from you these experiences. Yes, you are wounded, but you can heal and recover. You must hear this now. You will never return to your old selves. However, you can make peace with your new selves and learn to love again," Dor said, looking at each one of them.

"For all of you, you see your integrities as compromised. You are sick and disgusted by some of the actions you took and continue to endure. We will help you explore that. And you can trust us.

"We live in an occupied land, as our ancestors before us have struggled with. The powers in charge do not know what it is we really seek, nor do they understand what we can offer the world. We will help you learn how to reconcile living in a world that is not your own."

Yes, there were great things that occurred while they were away. The three children had a lifetime of experiences in Rome. They saw the world changing. Yet, they were all greatly wounded. Yael had been raped, and Eliza nearly so on two different occasions. Eliza and Caleb almost drowned. Caleb had killed men who did not deserve to die and, in his wrath, considered allowing men to drown. He considered murdering the emperor of the Roman Empire as an act of revenge, a lesson he had already learned was bad behavior.

"You are a resilient lot, you three. You could have all given up as most people your age do once they are overcome with adversity. Instead, you chose to rely on each other for literally everything. You have eaten, slept, cried, killed, been disrobed by the emperor, bathed, and traveled across the world with no adult guidance. Caleb was the arms and weapons of the group; Eliza—the treasurer; Yael—the helpmate and guide in times of uncertainty, who wanted everyone to get along. Two of you have begun expressing mutual affection. All of this, I saw, is a divine response to an evil circumstance. I can already see how Yahweh has His hand in your lives, but I also see how the enemy will take these things and turn them into evil. That is why I reprimanded Caleb for holding Yael's hand. The enemy can and will make this a weapon of evil. We are here to help you navigate this road," Rabbi Dor said.

"But for now, we shall all sleep. Each of you shall drink of this milk, and you will sleep deeply. When you are awake, come down and find each other. We are going to begin our healing journeys in the morning, and these will be intense sessions," he said. "You will all need the rest that this milk provides."

Once he was done, he called for one of their interns to come with a small hot cup of milk mixed with some sort of flower. They each drank of it and went to their rooms to sleep. Boys and girls remained separated, as is Hebrew tradition, and they slept without worries for the first time since they left this place over a month ago.

Yeshua was obviously using them for something big. They all knew it. They just did not know for what.

ON THE WALLS OF JERUSALEM

Once the administrator finished the intake process with everyone, two Roman centurions came dressed in their best regalia and lead the six women away to dinner. The Romans learned long ago that if the men could see that the women were fed and respected at mealtime, they were less explosive and less likely to cause problems or attempt an escape. This act was part of their risk management strategy to get the greatest value from their slaves. Centurions were considered the most honorable members of the military and the least likely to pillage and rape. Everyone knew that, and it made the men feel a bit safer than they otherwise might.

The task of retaining and maintaining a slave was as much a Roman financial commitment as it was a statement of power. Leadership within the empire concluded that attrition due to disease and malnutrition were preventable. Administrators demonstrated to leadership both in the Senate and within their legions that it was economically sound to train slave drivers how to get maximum longevity and productivity from their "tools" with behavior choices that do not include striking them at the first signs of deviation. In addition, the administrator got a bonus for completing the assigned public works project at or under budget, and he did everything he could to make slave management and efficiency a priority.

Katya walked next to one of the two well-clad centurions. From afar, she suspected that Matthew would be jealous if he saw her. She had no capacity to look back to see if he was there or to wave goodbye. She had no message for him other than, "I am safe."

The administrator broke Matthew's gaze on his departing wife.

"The centurions are escorting the women to a full dinner, followed by a tour of the facilities where they will be working. They will return to be with you before you sleep this night," said the administrator. He had an accent, and it was obvious Greek was his second language. Wherever he was from, Matthew thought it was possible that he, too, might be a slave. There was no way to figure that out unless he disclosed it. Matthew knew to wait to get to know him before asking such a question.

The first act the administrator did to earn their trust was to keep his promise. Katya and all the other women returned that evening. Husbands and wives were allowed to embrace and spend time alone, and each couple was given their own tent. History had shown that sexually active slaves were more predictable than ones who were forced to control their sex drives. Matthew questioned where Katya went, what she did, and what she learned of her new job. Matthew could not reciprocate with any details, as he had only been told that he was to report to the wall at sunrise. She told him of the large kitchen area and all the rotations of preparation, cooking, and cleaning that she would be a part of. Much of it reminded her of the mass meal preparation she did when she was younger with her sister when it was their turn to feed the village.

Of Healing and Finding Home

Matthew woke up in the middle of the night, almost in disbelief that his wife was still next to him. Her warm body next to his during the winter was most important when they lived in Correae near the Northerns. In Jerusalem, the milder climate kept the air warmer in the winter but not warm enough to sleep without his wife. He clung to her with a sense of gratitude that he was allowed to stay with her.

When the sun came up the next morning, they heard the call to exit and went to the administrator to get their cards. He repeated the charge to keep them at all times without repeating the consequences of losing them. It was a brief walk to the wall, and the men were all told to place their cloaks on a broken wagon near where they were to work. Each was assigned a partner, and each group of sixteen slaves was assigned a foreman. Overall, Matthew concluded that there were four foremen, meaning about sixty-four slaves were working in this area. Some groups were given shovels and gloves to protect their hands from infections that might slow down their work. Two were given water barrels and cups to carry with instructions not to spill any of it. Yet, most were given baskets that were held in place with a strap and padded cloth that went over their heads for efficiency when carrying the rubble and brick they were expected to move.

The men were shown a small kiln that was near capacity with recently finished bricks; their job for the day was to carry the bricks through one of the city gates to a construction site within the ancient city. There was another kiln near a different gate. Once they finished with this kiln in a few weeks, they would move to the other. They were told that the bricks were used for building residences inside the city walls, but nothing more than that. Matthew suspected that the foremen did not know what the structures were to be used for either, as they were not overseeing the construction.

Late in the morning, after carrying four loads of bricks from the kiln to the construction site, they were given a short break for water and bread. When the foreman said that it was time to go back to work, one of the men hesitated. The foreman did not speak to anyone but instead struck the man with a long thin iron stick that all foremen carried, and two soldiers began briskly walking towards the man who had faffed. Blood erupted from the site of the wound, and the slave turned in anger towards the foreman. Once he saw that the two soldiers were walking and looking at him only, he backed down. He was about to speak when the foreman lifted his iron rod, prompting the guards to unsheathe their gladii. He raised his hand to protect his head when the iron rod came down on his upper arm, injuring the underside but breaking no bones. Some dogs started barking when the man screamed, as that sound represented a potential dinner call for the military pets. All Roman slave stations included dogs; of the many purposes they served, dead slave disposal was one.

Over the next few days, some Jews resisted the Roman dominance, and their outcomes were the stuff of horror. Some of the other men in their group could not understand the broken Greek spoken by the foreman and experienced a far worse fate. Of the four foremen, two of them were from Gaul. If a Jew laughed out loud, the foremen concluded that they were making fun of them or their accent. From that moment until they breathed their last, the lives of the slaves were a downward spiral of physical and emotional abuse. It nearly always ended in death.

It started with a public beating administered by the foreman during a break. It was important for others to watch without interrupting their labor. His rod would not stop until the slave failed to respond to the last blow, meaning they had gone into shock. Many would lay there for the rest of the day until it was time to return to the tents. Any action other than attempting to return to work meant either no food at dinner or additional beatings on the already injured section of the body. For about half of the slaves, the first time this event occurred, they would keep a low profile, doing exactly what was expected of them and not speaking unless spoken to first. Getting off of the foreman's bad list was all that mattered to them, as they knew their body could not take repeated blows. Some slaves decided that they would not let the foreman break their morale, and they would fight back with passive-aggressive behavior. They would resist commands or offer scowls when reprimanded for poor deliveries.

"Keep acting like that and working like that, and you will make me some denarii as I sell you for a couple of lashings," the foreman might say. Then, they would act upon it both decisively and profitably. The foreman would agree upon a story that best described the ornery slave, and they would sell the rights to strike him with a whip four times for a denarius.

Other slaves would watch the transaction. Those lashings also happened only during breaks when the men were all resting and eating. The foreman would bring in the buyer and have other slaves hold the defiant slave. Although no slave ever died from the four lashings, many foremen would tell them they could get their coin back if they could kill them by the fourth hit. Although none died, the ferocity of the attacks created a deep fear that convinced many slaves to comply with all requests from the foreman.

Matthew's training as a screener for his village gave him great insight into the body language of the construction team. He learned that working constantly, even if only slowly, would get him the check on his card he needed for dinner.

Each night, his wife came back to be with him in his tent. She had been assigned to the kitchens, and she was allowed to bring home extras from there; they never went to bed hungry, as some of the others might. Although the Romans were only partially aware of Hebrew customs, they did allow the Seder meal, and they allowed them to travel inside the city to the place where the Temple used to be to stand at the remnants of the wall and pray weekly. Most importantly, they allowed the married couples to keep the privacy of their own tent, never having to share with another slave. For them, life as a slave was not bad. The Romans needed the majority to draw this conclusion to fuel their mass public works projects across the empire. At any given moment, as many as a quarter of all Jews were enslaved during the first century AD.

Just like Katya, Matthew prayed each day that their slavery would end soon, and they would find their Eliza.

For her part, Katya worked in a nearly all-women environment, preparing larger meals for the soldiers and slaves, and she served and cleaned up twice a day. They would start early and end late, but there was lots of time in the middle when they did not have any assignments when she could do tasks that any woman might. She washed clothes, bathed, cleaned her tent area, and would sit with friends, drinking tea and talking of their life before slavery. It was not that much different for her than life back home.

Yet, she also saw men come into the kitchen area and abduct one woman, and the woman never returned. More often, though, some woman would be taken once a week and bedded by several soldiers, specifically the ones that had been on patrol and encountered resistance. These men would take their anger out on the Jewish women as an act of retribution against Jewish men who would not do what was asked of them. Soldiers from other parts of the empire assumed that all Jews were of the same family and tribe, and the actions of one group applied to all of them. More than one defiant member of the tribe of Dan would cause a Levite to be raped. Katya told her husband about this, and he recommended that she keep a fresh onion near her at all times so that if a man did enter, she could begin slicing it immediately, subconsciously sending him to pick someone else who did not smell as pungent. She also volunteered for chamber pot duty, as well, knowing that the men did not want to have intercourse with a woman who carried feces and urine for disposal.

Katya saw one woman from a different slave group return after being gone for two days. Her face seemed normal, but both of her arms and legs were bruised, and she bled out from her loins. She was expected to immediately take her place in the kitchens, chopping up okra for all the other slaves and soldiers that evening, but she was too weak even to sit and chop. Katya and another woman walked her to her tent, covered her in a blanket, and laid her down. They closed the tent's canvas door and told the administrator that she was ill and was lying down. He nodded his head and told them to return to their duty stations.

The next morning, the woman was shaking, in septic shock, and unable to get out of bed, even to stand for a moment. The administrator asked about her condition, and after Katya shared her state, he sent all of the women to work, even though there was nothing to do in the kitchen at that time. When the women came back out to check on her a short time later, she was gone.

"She was a burden that we could not justify nor afford," was how the administrator described his choice to remove her. He would not answer any questions as to where he took her or what he did with her. The callous nature of Roman authority on display reminded Katya of what Yael described when she saw an older woman decapitated after she left Correae on her way to Jerusalem.

By the end of the first month, they were in a routine that seemed to work for them. Strange and unexpected as it may be, Katya and Matthew had not been this sexually active since they were newlyweds, nor had they spent this much time talking together late at night, as there were no distractions. Nor had they ever had such a great prayer life. Late one evening, Katya looked her husband in the eyes and spoke from the depths of her heart after a prayer.

"My love, if we leave this place and return, I want to continue this level of relationship with you. I want to spend every night in your arms, and I want to go to our bed early, not staying up late and talking to the village. I am closer to you now than at any time in my life with you," she said.

Matthew nodded and agreed.

"You are wise, old woman," he said.

"I am not that old, Matthew. After all, I am again with child," she said. And with that sweet and touching announcement, the two of them embraced and said another prayer. Matthew allowed tears to flow freely, and Katya looked at her husband and smiled, happy to be his wife, experiencing his total acceptance and his total transparency.

"Yeshua uses all things for His glory. I tell you the truth: this child shall also be His glory, just as the older sister who came before," Matthew said, lightly touching his wife, their ankle bands striking during the intimate moment, reminding them that their physical bodies were enslaved, but their hearts belonged to each other.

THE VOLUNTEERS AT THE HOUSE OF HEALING

The milk worked as Rabbi Dor told it would, and they all woke up feeling rested. When they came downstairs, there was a loaf of fresh bread and several boiled eggs laid out for them. Caleb ate six eggs and half a loaf all by himself, and Zev ate his food outside with his daughter. No one dared to join them, as that was the first time Yael and Zev had father/daughter time in over a year. Caleb took off hunting before he finished his last bite, leaving Eliza alone. She was not ready to be alone, so she spent the unstructured time speaking with many of the volunteers, many of whom she had not met. The last time she was here, the only people's names she remembered were the rabbis' and the only words she remembered were those of the rabbis. Yet, for every rabbi, there were five to ten volunteers. With no rabbis in sight, Eliza tackled her loneliness with new people and new conversation.

She was almost in disbelief as she learned that many of the servant volunteers were esteemed leaders in their local communities who were here as part of trauma counseling training. None were paid, and they all covered the costs of their own room and board while there were in attendance. The Roman occupation had made atrocities and crimes against humanity so commonplace that nearly every synagogue in occupied Judah doubled as a hospital for the emotionally wounded. The need for spiritual guides with a foundation in inner healing was immense, and there were few places in Judah where such instruction was possible. Eliza already knew that this house was a place where those who had been injured could come for restoration. What she did not know was that it was a school for others to learn how to orchestrate that magical task.

As she listened to all their stories and learned how each group chose to come here, she imagined if these feelings of awe and wonder were the same ones her aunt felt when she uncovered the tunnel underneath Jerusalem some fifteen years earlier. Neither she nor her aunt expected such emotional morsels alongside real-world blessings.

The first group of volunteers she got to know was the kitchen staff. The dishwasher, the firewood gatherer, and the oven assistant were men who owned estates near the coast where refugees came ashore. All of them were wealthy landowners outside the ancient city of Gaza, and the currents in the Mediterranean brought boats ashore near their properties all the time. These men shared anecdotal stories of the ships full of victims of Roman village burnings that would come ashore and walk towards their estates, as theirs were the only buildings in sight. Hearing that they had nowhere else to turn, their staff would greet these refugees and honor their pleas for assistance. As was Hebrew custom, they would offer them a place to stay and some food. As word of the unexpected arrivals reached the owners, they would walk down the hillside to meet these new and uninvited residents of their land. As the refugees told the owners their stories, their hearts would break.

After several iterations of hearing the heartfelt requests for a new life from these arriving refugees, it was decided at

Of Healing and Finding Home

one of their monthly landowner meetings that they needed a community response. Although all of them could offer seasonal jobs to them in their olive orchards and wheat fields, none of them could offer them the help they needed to heal from the ravages they experienced. After a few months of inclusion on the management meeting docket, they took a vote. They agreed that each house needed to send their leaders to partake in this hands-on volunteer-based training to address the needs of what they all concluded were society's most vulnerable members. Eliza shook her head in disbelief that the bakers who woke up in the dark of night to make sure that they had fresh bread as they started their healing journey owned as much land as her entire hometown of Correae.

This group of middle-aged men were on their second stint as volunteers there, and they were moved beyond words at what they saw happening in the house. All the men wore normal clothing and spoke street Hebrew; however, all of them had been briefed by Rabbi Benji after the four guests had drunk their warm milk, and they all knew who Eliza was. She was the girl who ministered to the emperor and was embraced for the power of her teachings. They all poured upon her praise and affirmations to let her know how her risk had impacted them in their faith. She blushed as many of these men extended the gratitude.

"Oh, my lords! I am humbled to meet you," she said, unable to keep her focus. How could men like this humble themselves to serve a girl like her? She felt that she should be serving them.

"We are glad you had the wisdom to come here. As men of great wealth, we, too, are humbled. You wield unfathomable power by possessing that ring that you wear. You could easily exceed any of our accomplishments, yet you stand here, awaiting Rabbi Dor to submit to him. You are a mystery to us, and we are grateful to serve you," one of the men said.

"We are watching a butterfly emerge from its cocoon. That is what I think," said another, as some of them laughed lovingly.

A few of them saw that she was uncomfortable receiving all this praise, and one offered her a path to depart. "We are here to make the rabbi's job easier. You can act as if we are not here, and we will not be offended," one of them shared, as none of them wanted to impact her healing journey.

Eliza was at a loss for words. She reflected back to the story of the three kings who came to visit baby Yeshua. They were men of immense authority and resources, yet they humbled themselves to travel a distance to worship. She could see that these men were replicating the example set before them only two generations ago, and the thought left her shaking her head. She wondered how her aunt might react in this moment. As she did, another landowner who had the most experience with the refugees continued their story.

The estate owners started with an agreement amongst themselves to spend two weeks in residence and go back and discuss their experiences at the following month's management meeting. At that first meeting back, they agreed to send their wives on the next trip. The men saw that many who came were women who had survived sexual assault and rape and that they appeared to need the most help. Eliza learned that one of those women was the wife of the current dishwasher. Based on descriptions, she remembered Eliza. Six weeks ago, Eliza was known as the cousin of the boy who had lost his parents and killed the Roman centurion in charge of the strike force.

"My bride told me about your family's tragedy when she came home, and my entire estate prayed for you. After

Of Healing and Finding Home

the tales we heard about you and your cousin last night, all of us smiled and shook our heads at how Jehovah Jireh answers our prayers. The Messiah is certainly using you, Little One," he said.

The back-and-forth banter continued. Eliza imagined them having this level of conversational sharing as they discussed their finances. She was blessed to be trusted with transactional execution for her village of a hundred families. These men's crops filled a thousand boats full of olives each year and another twice that in wheat. They employed thousands, and she was in awe at the immense power they wielded. Their tithes were responsible for the continuation of Hebrew culture in an occupied land full of enslavement and crimes against humanity. All the while, they were Yeshuaians, and she had no idea. Money had always been associated with sin in her people's history. These men were obviously proving that the past does not dictate the present. They were now serving her, and that thought could not find a place that these diametric beliefs could fit in her mind.

"Can I ask you to tell us a story if you do not mind? Can you tell us about your conversation with the emperor? We heard that he invited you to the palace and asked you to remain and teach him more about the Messiah. What was that like?" a man asked.

With that, she recounted the story of leaving the Colosseum and receiving an invite to the palace. Eliza told them that as she readied for the evening that she knew may include forced participation in an orgy, she felt a peace come over her that she would not be harmed that day. When the emperor came to her, she found it natural and easy talking to him about her uncle and his former best friend, and the words of his friend Rufus softened his heart. Whoever the man was before their late-night meeting was no one that she knew. However, the man afterward was open to allowing the idea of a loving Yahweh to rule his heart and rule his empire. She told all the volunteers how empty she felt when she learned that he died less than three days later, and it gave her an extra hunger to get here.

"We have all prayed that one day the emperor would get to know the Messiah for who He is, not as a man who posed a threat to our people. You were an answer to that prayer, Little One. In the same way that Yahweh sent our Savior to be born in a manger, I tell you now, Yahweh continues to work in mysterious ways. Just when we think that we understand the Yahweh of Abraham, Isaac, and Jacob, we meet someone like you, and we see that we are all fools. He sent a teenage girl to minister to the emperor and anointed her words to touch his heart. This is unfathomable to us. I tell you now, we all think of you as a page in our people's history," they said. She could only smile. These accolades were undeserved in her mind.

"Titus and I talked about the mystery of Yeshua and Yahweh being one. Titus was a man with an empty soul and knew he needed a savior. I was able to tell him what was in his soul that he did not see."

With that, none could speak. The men looked at each other and nodded their heads in disbelief at what they had just heard. There was nothing more any could add. They offered her some more tea, but she declined and left.

She proceeded into the main room. She met a group of women from the Golan Heights responsible for all housekeeping and grounds clean-up. They traveled together on foot for nearly a week to reach this place. They had sent a message asking permission to come around the same time Eliza and Caleb were here last, and it was immediately granted. They were currently nearing the end of their stay, and they shared that another group from their village was coming after them to replace them in their service to the house.

Eliza inquired where they were from. When they told her that their hometown was Har Meron, she almost jumped out of her chair, as that part of the Golan Heights was only a day's journey from Correae; however, she still felt an obligation to bite her tongue and not tell them. Her village's gold had to remain a secret.

Har Meron's need was similar to that of the men from Gaza. They had been flooded with refugees coming inland from Tyre and Canaan after their villages were damaged or destroyed by Roman soldiers. Many in Canaan attempted to rebel against Roman authority, as was Canaanite tradition, but they were beaten down and evicted from their homes. They would travel overland in small groups, often experiencing attrition as they crossed portions of land that lacked any rule of law. In addition to the loss of their homes and family croplands, many of them were robbed of their family's heirlooms as they crossed the unirrigated plains of Canaan. Many of the older members of these extended families died before they would make it to the walled city of Har Meron.

Once inside the city walls, the community development workers quickly discovered that they did not have enough resources to help the emotional needs of these foreigners. They were poor, to begin with, and the trip across the country on foot left most of them malnourished and weak. Food and shelter were easy for the community development workers to address; however, the real problems began to emerge as the refugees told them of the atrocities that they had experienced. No amount of food and employment could help them with the impact those events had on them, and they lived a haunted life. Their village had selected these women to come and observe how the rabbis interfaced with injured souls, so they could return home and share what they learned.

Before Caleb returned from his morning hunt, Rabbi Dor entered the main room. He greeted Eliza, and she addressed him using the royal honorific form of language. The rabbi gestured to bring in the men from the kitchen, and they joined the women from Har Meron to pray. Even in the presence of a properly trained rabbi, Eliza thought nothing of adding to the prayer, thanking Yeshua that all these wealthy men were Yeshua's followers. When they finished the prayer, Dor told her that they would spend the rest of the morning outside. She stepped out and decided she did not need a cloak, so they proceeded to the gardens behind the main structure. Then, Eliza began to tell him her story of what haunted her.

ELIZA AND YAEL TELL THEIR STORIES

Eliza had desperately looked forward to stepping on a boat and leaving the harbor in Rome. She had too many emotional experiences here and needed to be away from it. The moment she felt the boat pull away from the docks made her wonder if this was how her ancestors felt when Yahweh told them to leave the land that was the source of all of their oppression and begin their journey to the promised land. For sure, Rome was the ultimate land of oppression, and she could only see Judah as her promised land.

She did not know if it was divine providence or the power of the emperor that had the three of them sailing within moments of reaching the docks; either way, she could not be more grateful. The ship immediately caught a strong wind pulling them out of sight of all the Roman ports before mid-day. She closed her eyes and turned her face into the cold winter wind, grateful beyond words both that they had come to the city to save her parents and grateful they left without any physical harm.

She and Yael sat down at the front of the boat, staring at the coast of the province of Italy to their left. It was much more colorful than Judah, and it would be there for three full days before they would turn east and traverse the strait of Messina and have nothing but open water for a week. The sea waves rocked them as they traveled downwind while the waves of emotion began to take over her soul and sense of self.

She pondered her conclusions that they had a safe and harm-free visit, and she saw that she was wrong. Yes, they all were physically undamaged; however, they were not unharmed. She had hidden from herself the truth that she was held down by several strange men who tried to take off her undergarment and violate her. She had not allowed herself to feel what she experienced when the emperor had disrobed her and exposed her upper body to a crowd of 50,000 while demanding her cousin kill two men to protect and save them. Yet, her mind could not stop repeating the filthy words used by other royalty as they waited in line to enter the Colosseum as they spoke about her partially exposed body in vulgar terms. She could not compartmentalize all these events and feel peace. Indeed, she was haunted by nightmares daily.

She remained a young virgin girl from Judah. She was not meant to be sexual at such a young age—that was what all of her elders taught her. The men of the Roman Empire thought otherwise, and she only now understood why their message of fidelity before marriage was so important. Yes, her aunt had fornicated before marriage, and the first time she did so of her volition. It altered her irrevocably. For Eliza, all of her sexual exposure was forced upon her, and she felt betrayed. Indeed, she felt dirty and ashamed.

As the gravity of these events set in, Eliza was frazzled and could do nothing other than hold Yael and look around to make sure Caleb was nearby. As she let herself start to feel the shame of her condition, she wept bitterly. She felt just as much pain for Caleb as he was forced to commit an atrocity of the most extreme nature when he killed other followers of Yeshua to protect her and Yael. How did he reconcile this? He took the dagger and slit the throats of two men who called Yeshua the Messiah, even with their last breaths. He held up their heads as they bled out, refusing to look down as they breathed their last. How could Caleb be okay?

Paradoxically, she wondered how she could ever exist without him in her life. Since the first attack on Tamar, she felt bound to him, but now she needed more than he could offer her.

Yael had a similar emotional tidal wave. For the first time, Yael began to speak of what male members of the House of Caesar did to her body that she had not known was possible, and she felt equally dirty. She talked about walking through the city, thinking that everyone could see the scars these men made upon her as they treated her as a piece of property. She talked about how she would bathe herself repeatedly, hoping the water would wash not just her body but her soul. Life as a slave meant a life without freedom, and until that freedom was lost, it was impossible to convey its impact. She had experienced the sickness of the Roman Empire both at the palace and the Colosseum, and the images that were burned into her memory were too powerful for her to push away.

Fortunately, the boat was nearly empty, and Eliza and Yael could sit on the main deck after the sunset in their warm cloaks and scarves and allow each other the opportunity to weep tears that should have long since come out. After a few days, their tears turned to whimpers until there were no more tears to be shed. As the days passed, Yael and Eliza repeated the tales of what they experienced, finding that they had missed a key detail. Too many times, each of them started their conversation with the phrase, "I have never said this to anyone, but," as they allowed light to be shined in the dark places that had created an identity of shame. Magic happened as they shared, and the power these secrets had over them began to wane. It took every minute of the ride down the coast to talk them through.

In her heart, Eliza knew from its greatest depths that Yeshua had kept all His promises by bringing her away from that despot of evil. Yael concluded the same thing in her own way. Both could not wait to get home, thinking that home would erase the damage. Yael missed her family, and she wanted to see her little sister. She never wanted her to experience this.

Before they reached land, Eliza opened the scroll that Emperor Titus gave her and read it for the first time. Yael could not read and write Greek like Eliza could, so Eliza read it out loud:

> *All authority and resources of our Great Roman Empire are to be considered at the disposal of Eliza of Correae from northern Judah. Release to her or her designate both Katya and Matthew from Correae. Any debt due for their release shall be considered forfeit and canceled. No man may read this letter and not respond without forfeiting their life to the sword of Caleb of Tamar.*
>
> *Titus Flavian, Emperor of Rome*

The decree was dated and covered in some sort of protective oil that prevented the ink from running or the papyrus from degrading in the presence of water.

"Wow, that sounded like some of the other decrees that he has written for members of the Senate. You really impacted him!" said Yael. Eliza smiled and handed the letter to Caleb to read. As he took it from her hand, she rested her forehead in her right hand and allowed more tears to flow. She did not know that the emperor was still controlling Caleb, even after they left Rome. Caleb maintained a role in enforcing the letter she so desperately sought that left him susceptible to additional required killings. He needed to read it for himself and see that she was not teasing him. She wished she hadn't asked Titus for the letter. Caleb was livid.

"Eliza, this is not okay. I am done with killing. Do you hear me? I can't do that, again, not for you and not for anyone! I have listened to you two these last few days, and I am glad you two can talk. I can't! My predicament is not the same as yours. You two will never desire to be sexually assaulted; of that point, I am sure. The emperor wants me to exercise my skills and kill again. He has set us up! I don't know what to do about it. When you get to the end of the note when you read it, please omit that last sentence. Would you do that for me?" he asked. Once he had said it, he walked to the other side of the boat and looked across the water. He stayed near enough to both of them so they could see him and feel safe. It was obvious only now that he was equally seeking help from what he had seen and done. Rome had wounded them all.

"What can we do to help him with his suffering?" asked Yael.

"He knows that there are people at the House of Healing who can help him navigate this. And I can omit that last sentence. Most soldiers cannot read, anyway," she said. The two nodded.

"I hope he does not go back to Rome and take that job the emperor offered him," said Yael. "If he does, he will never heal, and this will become his destiny," she said.

"I think you are right," said Eliza.

And with that last piece of the story, Rabbi Dor smiled.

"Little One, that is a lifetime of experience in only a month of elapsed time. Yahweh certainly thinks you are strong enough to handle this. I do not know what I might have done if I were in any of your shoes," he said. He intentionally waited for those words to soak in before proceeding. He extended her soul a moment of grace with small talk, then he returned to information gathering and asked her lots of questions. It was then that she noticed there were three women working the gardens near to them, listening with the intent of learning how to do what Dor was doing. Dor spoke up.

"Eliza, I want to show you something."

Dor handed her a small but polished mirror, and the women working in the garden walked to her but stayed a few steps away. They needed to watch Dor and learn.

"Inside of it is what only you can describe. Let's start with that for now, okay?" Dor asked her. She nodded in agreement. Their teacher/student relationship picked up right where they left it when they were last together.

"Well, it's me!" she said. She knew Dor enough to know that if she did not keep talking, he would make her talk.

"Describe her, please," he asked.

"So, it is a young woman who has seen too much," she said, allowing some tears to fall from her face. She wiped them away quickly, feeling embarrassed that these unknown women were watching her.

"Last time we spoke, you talked of your desire to explore and travel more than returning home to Correae. Much of that prayer has been answered, yes? You now have seen a lot. Now, you also say you have seen too much. Talk about that. What you wanted seems to contradict what you experienced," he said in the gentlest of voices.

He was right, and she did not know it until that moment. She began to answer him, looking up at him on occasion.

"Tell this to the person in the mirror. They need to hear from you, as they are the person with the most experience," he said. With that, she would return to the mirror, talking to, what Dor wanted her to conclude, was her friend. She told the person in the mirror many things, but at the end, she began to see that the person in that polished material was, in fact, her friend.

"That person in the mirror wants to get to know you, Little One. You cannot hide from her and be okay," he said. She nodded, pondering the immenseness of the meaning of Dor's words. She had buried her emotions and saw that the effort damaged her as much as the experience did.

"Your new friend, do you see her?" he asked. She slowly nodded and agreed. "Just like you want Yael to get to know the real you, the same is true for the person in that mirror. They want to know the real you. Keep that mirror. Remember to take it out when you experience loss and pain like that again. Okay?" he asked. With that lesson complete, Dor and Eliza practiced talking to the girl in the mirror with other difficult questions to make sure Eliza understood how to use it.

As they finished their time outdoors, Eliza found that she was both tired and sleepy. Caleb had already come back and was outside writing something down, but she did not stop to talk to him. She went in and was immediately served a meal with lots of tasty vegetables and pickled fruits. The food was better than anything she had eaten in the last three weeks. She thanked the preparers and ate her full. She returned to her room to nap. As she lay in bed and began dozing off, she thanked Yeshua for Yael. Eliza had a sister of greater worth than gold or silver, and it was her turn to heal.

And, for the first time, she thanked Yeshua for the person in that mirror.

YAEL'S FIRST DAY IN THE HOUSE OF HEALING

Dor watched Eliza walk off to take a nap, and he found Yael. It was her turn, now. They spent a considerable period of time with small talk, as he wanted to know more about her family story and tales of her childhood. He got to know the names of some of her friends and asked some additional questions about her time in Rome unrelated to her abuse. Then, he knew he needed to focus on what troubled her.

"Let's talk about what happened to you when the Caesar man assaulted you. You omitted much of the details of that story. It is important you learn to speak of those details, and you need some place where this is safe to practice. To help you feel safe, I have asked some of the housekeeping staff to sit and listen to us," he said, gesturing for three women who stood at a distance to come and join them.

"For now, these women will listen and pray while we talk. They are here to help you, and everything you say shall be considered sacred," he said.

With that, Yael told of how the Caesar man took her to a bathing pool and committed filthy acts with her while other slaves watched and served him wine. She tried speaking up to tell the man to stop, but she was pummeled until she stopped talking. The man finished his acts with her then told her to get up and leave, almost immediately. Yael stared into the distance and recounted details that she thought she would never speak of, pausing to wipe tears from her eyes as she described her horror. All the while, her mouth remained open, as her breathing became short and shallow. After a time, she found that she had no events or experiences left inside of her that were hidden.

As he pressed her for details on what she learned, he saw that she was making many incorrect connections. Specifically, she was connecting intimacy with pain and pleasing a man with being dominated. She needed to know that those were not true conclusions.

"Do you ever think your father did that to your mother?" he asked.

"No!" she said.

"You are correct. Let me ask you this. Before this act that you were forced to take part in, how should a man love his wife?" he asked.

She bashfully answered. When done, Dor spoke up again.

"I want you to hear from these three women. Because this activity is sacred in our culture, I will not be present to hear what you say. I will stand by the fireplace and await one of you to wave for me to return. I will pray while you share with each other."

After Dor walked away, he began humming a prayer that she had heard many times in Hebrew school. It made her smile and reminded her of safety. Then, each of the three women shared intimate stories as to how their husbands engaged them and attempted to please them. They told her how they, in turn, pleased their husbands. Hebrew culture has always had shortcomings with the lack of sexual instruction from older women to younger women, and these women were aware of that. They answered every one of Yael's questions gently, and all of them often covered their faces as they laughed at things Yael had been taught that she "should not talk about." As they came near the end, all of the women told Yael that what was done to her was neither right nor something she should ever expect to experience from a loving man. The women told Yael to wave to Dor to come back.

As soon as he arrived, he asked her nothing of their conversation but proceeded to the next teaching.

"Tell me, what is the fate of a goose who flies away from the flock?" he asked.

"It gets lost, perhaps, and many other things," she said. Dor asked her a series of additional questions, all exposing the value of a group staying together not just for survival but for thriving and growing.

"Do you wish to marry and have children one day?" he asked.

"Yes," Yael said.

"Then I tell you the truth: our people have a protocol for marriage that protects our purity and follows Yahweh's will for marriage. You must be like the geese who want to succeed and fly with the flock. Tell me: what do you think that means for you?" he asked.

"I should not succumb to the same temptations as Caleb's mother," she answered. The rabbi was not thinking of that answer, but it was appropriate. He nodded and laughed as he saw the irony of her choice to select one of his teachers to be the example not to follow.

"What are some steps you can take to make sure that this does not happen to you?" he asked.

She had a long pause before she answered.

"I must first enter into erusin with a man willing to build a home for our future family before I engage in—" she said before he interrupted.

"Before you engage is not correct. Before you allow yourself to engage is a better use of words. You had no choice in Rome. Now, you have a choice. This lesson is very important. You were a victim. You are not anymore. You can make choices. Let me teach you how to do that. Would you like that?" he said.

And with that, he began a series of simple exercises to help her see the differences between having no choice and having a choice. They practiced seeing the difference when she was allowing guilt to make choices instead of her whole being. Lastly, they role-played some choices that he perceived she might have to make in the near future. When they finished, it was time to prepare for dinner, and the women had to leave. Yael went back to their room and found Eliza just waking up. They had a lot to talk about.

CALEB'S ANSWER

Rabbi Benji knew that Caleb was poor at identifying feelings when compared to the girls. However, Caleb was also faster than the girls at performing actions requiring courage. Their first exploration of Caleb's nightmares was either going to be short and fast or was going to take longer than anyone else's.

Rabbi Benji interrogated Caleb about all the events that had transpired since they were last together. He was able to get Caleb to detail the torments from his killings on the boat and in the Colosseum. Caleb's pain hit a crescendo when he told Benji what the last sentence of the emperor's decree said and how he asked Eliza not to read it.

"Caleb, my boy, do you remember the last time you were here?" the rabbi asked.

"Yes, Benji," he said. Benji did not much think that the words "Rabbi Benjamin" needed to be used every time Caleb spoke to him, so he gave him permission to shorten it.

"What lesson did you take from here before any of the other events you talked about began to happen?" he asked.

"Vengeance is the possession of Jehovah Jireh," the boy said.

"That is correct. We had another item of interest to cover. What was the opposite of vengeance?" Benji asked.

"I do not remember talking about that," Caleb said with complete sincerity.

"We never did. However, it came up on the boat ride. What is the opposite of vengeance?" he repeated.

"Forgiveness?" the boy said, smiling.

Benji knew his student. He raised his fist and pumped.

"Yes," he said, "Good job!" He knew Caleb needed to talk about his struggle with vengeance.

"I was absolutely ready to kill all of the men who were attempting to harm Eliza."

Benji laughed.

"And you think you sinned when you did that?"

"Yes, I did sin!" Caleb answered emphatically.

"When Yeshua entered the Temple half a century ago, he had a similar experience. He saw something built and meant to serve and be pleasing to Yahweh being defiled by human greed. When you saw Yahweh's creation, whom you call Cousin Eliza, about to defiled, you made it clear that such action was no different than greed. Jesus turned over tables and tossed the perpetrators aside; he did not talk to them and politely ask them to desist. I tell you the truth: that day, your heart was the same as the Messiah's," Benji said, placing his hand on Caleb's shoulder, looking the young man in the eye.

"Then why do I feel that I have sinned?" he asked.

"Caleb, that was not vengeance. You were protecting your family in the same way a mother bear swings her paw and decapitates a man for getting too close to her cubs. Most boys your age would only yell or perhaps strike the evil in those men with their fists. You shot them to save the ones you love. That act is not full of malice. It is self-defense. Your cousin represents a part of yourself.'"

"But I was really angry when I shot at the men trying to rape Eliza. Was that not sin?" he asked. Benji began laughing, and he hugged Caleb repeatedly as he did it.

"I love you, young man. I sincerely love you," he said, waiting to control himself.

"If anger is sin, then Yeshua sinned," he said. He knew he needed to give Caleb a puzzle to keep his mind engaged.

Caleb shook his head. He knew that was not right.

"Anger isn't sin, then. So what did I do that was sin?" he asked.

"You tell me," Benji demanded.

"I did not sin, then?" Caleb said.

"I do not believe that you *mean* that," said Benji.

"What?" said Caleb in disbelief.

"Say that you like you mean it!" said Benji, standing up and raising his voice.

"I did not sin," Caleb repeated, but without much emotion.

"Say it again. This time, say it like you mean it. Say it like you were talking to Zev the moment you met him," said Benji. Caleb smiled. He stood up. He had no weapon on him, but if he had a sword, he would have unsheathed it.

"I did not bloody sin! I was defending my family from harm!" he said.

"Okay, I want you to go inside and tell everyone in the kitchen that you did not sin and that you were defending yourself and your family; then tell everyone in the dining room. Then I want you to go to the backyard and write down that you were defending your family against an attacker and that this is not sin. Write this down three times. Then, bring it to me," said Benji.

Caleb immediately got up and left. Benji knew the young man's resolve. He knew both of his parents, and he knew his uncle. This would be over quickly.

While Caleb did what was asked of him, Benji went to find Zev.

OF ZEV

Benji was younger than Zev, but he was a rabbi, and Zev was more than comfortable submitting to his authority. Zev knew from watching and listening to his daughter that he needed to be here. This was the least he could do for her to try to make things right.

It helped that Benji spent nearly no time with Caleb. He started working with Zev much earlier than he hoped for, and he was able to get to know the established Hebrew farmer before he initiated questions that he knew would disrupt his view of himself.

Benji quickly learned that Zev had not yet spoken to any adults about his self-loathing as to how he treated his daughter. No one knew that he hated himself for selling her into slavery, and he had been carrying that weight for over a year. In addition, Zev told no one about his shame of treating her poorly when she returned, partly because he left to come here. Most of the reasons were the same reasons he never talked about her slavery. Benji knew this man needed to return to a state of balance with his view of himself.

"Zev, we are going to make some lists. Let's start with all the things that you did wrong. What are they?" asked Benji.

"I sold my daughter into slavery, and it damaged her in ways that I did not understand," he said.

Benji said nothing while Zev wiped another tear from his eye. He continued.

"I gave up hope. I started drinking too much alcohol. I became lazy in my circumstance," he said. "I treated her like filth when she returned."

As he neared the end and had no other words to add, Benji decided that the opposite side of the coin was missing both in their conversation and this man's heart.

"Zev, take this coin. Tell me what you see?" he asked.

"The face of Titus is on one side, and him sitting is on the back," Zev said.

"Can you have a coin with only one side? Is that possible?" Benji asked.

"Of course not!"

"In the same way that a coin cannot have one side, so is it with a man," he said, allowing a few moments for that to settle while he rubbed the man's shoulder.

"Zev, let's make the next list, shall we? This time, I want you to tell me what you have done right?"

"What I have done right?"

"Yes, tell me about what you have done right, Zev."

Zev broke eye contact and jumped in with his answers.

"Marrying Yael's mother was my best decision. She was wonderful in every way, was truly a woman that Solomon himself would have been proud of. Next, having children with her and supporting them until the marauders came was also good. We removed forests together and made fields for crops, and all of us were proud of that advancement. Our community was better off for it. We kept a clean house nearly all of our lives, and our family was healthy until the end," he paused.

"I am glad that I listened to the village elders who suggested I spend coin from the harvest to educate my daughter.

Of Healing and Finding Home

That coin was very hard-earned, but it has served her well. She told me on the way here that she loved going to synagogue in Rome and reading the scrolls and writings of the rabbi. It connected her back to home when the sickness of life in the royal palace was taking her hope. Yes, I provided education for my daughter, even though many in the village did not. I helped with village affairs and worked on the irrigation team for our village," he said.

"Which list is longer?" asked Benji.

Zev did not speak.

"Zev, based on my counting, it looks like you have four negatives and countless positives on your ledger. If I were an accountant, would I find you to be in debt or have a surplus?" he asked.

"Surplus," Zev answered.

"Good. I am sure that your daughter agrees with that. Let's ask her later, okay?" the rabbi asked.

He could tell that Zev was scared to do this.

"You remain her father, yet you are scared. Why is this?"

The question demanded an answer.

"Because I think she will see only the bad."

"Does a person who sees more bad than good come home with a purse of coin and run into her childhood home to receive the love of her father?"

Zev did not speak.

"I just met Yael yesterday. It is apparent to all of us that she continues to honor you and has not forsaken you. Who does that sound like?" he asked.

"I know," Zev said. He saw it now. His daughter was behaving like a Yeshua follower. Bitter tears came from him now as he saw the folly of his thinking. Benji pulled him and let him cry. After a few moments, Benji pushed him away, and the two looked at each other face to face.

"All of us have prayed about this since we met you. Yahweh Himself is attempting to offer you a chance to heal. We need to share with you what we see happening and guide you. All of us are excited to see how you use this moment to heal!" he said. He waited for a nod of approval from Zev before continuing.

"Unless we have been deceived, young Eliza is reaching out to you like a father. Do you not see this?" he asked.

More tears fell from Zev's eyes as he looked down.

"She does."

"Yet, you have not accepted this love and have not accepted her as your daughter in your heart, have you?" he asked. Zev remained silent.

"I do not think you have. I do not think you believe you are deserving of this honor," said Benji. He spoke with compassion but also with the intention of piercing and exposing the man's fragile heart.

"No, not yet," he said.

"Should you do something about this?" Benji asked. This time, he gave Zev no time to answer.

"I tell you now: this is a great gift, sent by the Maker of the heavens and earth for you. It is the answer to your prayers to get your family back, I am sure of it."

Before Zev could answer, Benji shined light onto the darkness in a new way.

"If I had a daughter, I would make things right with her by any tool I could find. After all, one day, she will be a mother, a wife, a partner, and potentially a leader of many. Not only are you being given a chance to restore yourself with your first daughter, but Yahweh is also giving you a second one! Can you see this gift, Uncle?" he intentionally ended with a family expression, knowing that people remember the last thing they hear more than they do the first.

"It is obvious that Eliza will be a leader, yes, I agree," Zev said.

"Do you think a great leader needs a great father?" asked Benji. He did not allow him to answer, but instead, he told him that they were going for a walk to his favorite place near the top of the hill behind them. Once they reached Benji's happy place, Benji took out a blanket and laid it on top of some rocks where they would sit.

"You should know these things before I assign a task for you. Eliza's aunt was the first female rabbi in the history of our people. Do you know her name? It was Yael! She was also one of my teachers. If I was to tell you the truth, she was my best teacher. She was a woman among men, and she had to prove herself more than any man ever would. She did that with powerful teaching. In fact, nearly every method of instruction I have used with you today came from what I learned with her. Did you know that? She bears the same name as your daughter, Zev. She spoke to Paul and to Luke, and she transcribed many copies of the words of our Messiah and spread them across the world. By all measures, she is a true saint," he said. He shifted positions so Zev could see every part of his language, both spoken and unspoken, as Benji knew the power of a moment.

"Eliza's aunt invested more time and more words in Eliza than any woman who was ever in her life. As sure as I am talking to you, she will be a leader of many and more. She is already a history maker. Zev, you have been given a gift beyond words to be taken in as her father. You need to draw her in and accept her with unconditional love. You must not keep her away by only extending words. She deserves more than what you have done."

Zev broke eye contact and stared down the hill and into the heart of Kedron. The city was bustling with activity, and people were going about their affairs. He knew he was above them in the moment, able to see their group motions. He was also seeing his own motions, and he could see there was a need for change.

"She is knocking on your door with great risk of rejection, but she persists. I think you both need each other right now," Benji said.

"You have been forgiven by both your daughters for all that you have done. You need to accept their forgiveness. They have blessed you with a supernatural gift."

Zev was uncomfortable, as Benji's words demanded that he act. After Zev agreed that he needed to change his behavior, the two of them brainstormed several ideas as to how to show his daughters that he loved them unconditionally. Benji knew that action is a requirement on any man's healing journey.

"I think the winter is finally over. Today is warm. The cold of winter is over," Zev said, trying to make small talk.

Perfect, Benji thought.

"Time for you to act on the warmth that you are feeling now. Do not let this moment only be about the weather."

Zev stared straight ahead. He knew what he needed to do next.

SNACK IN THE NIGHT

Caleb and Zev shared a dorm room, and Zev was asleep when Caleb entered. During late winter and early spring, the length of the day increased rapidly, and the longer days brought much happiness to a people who spent most of their lives outside. Caleb had just finished his late-night counseling session with Benji and came up to the room. He could not sleep. He was excited not only from what he had just learned but also from what he saw. He found ostrich tracks in the afternoon, and he planned to hunt them in the morning. His tossing in the bed woke Zev up, and Caleb told Zev of his excitement. Both of them agreed that they were hungry. Caleb knew that the kitchen always had food on the counter, and the two of them got dressed, lit the candle, and walked down the hall to the kitchen.

None of the staff were awake, but the bread dough from last night was still rising on the counter. The oven was always fired with hot coals, so Caleb took a piece of the dough and put it in the oven to bake. Then, the men began to talk.

"Uncle, I love this kitchen. I come down here probably once a day, maybe more. They always have tasty food on the counter," said Caleb, trying to start a conversation. He found an apple bin as well as more oranges.

"I have not been hungry all week, it seems," said Zev. "I have been well fed, and I have greatly enjoyed my time here with Benji. I am grateful that you invited me to join you. I thought I lost everything. Seeing how you and your cousin have taken in my Yael leaves me speechless in gratitude."

Zev needed to follow up on Benji's strong suggestion to act and start healing. He was nervous, but he was resolute in what he needed to do. His daughter deserved it, and he and Benji had discussed it at length.

"Young man, why did you commit to protecting my daughter in that moment? I have considered my words before speaking, and your only obligation was to Eliza, not to my Yael. At that point, you had only known her one afternoon, and you took her publicly to be your sister," he said, staring at the young man. "And you did so before the emperor of Rome himself!"

Caleb looked away for a moment before responding.

"I do not know, really. It seemed like the right thing to do. My mother and father had just offered their lives for people who were not family; it seemed like the correct choice in the moment. An old man Barnabus used to come to our house to eat and bathe and talk to my dad. He used to say that there is no greater love than to lay down your life for your friends. I guess I thought that he was right," he said.

"So, you do love my daughter," said Zev.

Caleb snorted and smiled. "Yes, I guess I do," he shared.

"Who were your parents? Everyone we meet seems to know them but me. Benji has told me of your mother. Tell me more," Zev asked.

"My father was a rabbi in training in Jerusalem when the Temple was destroyed. He became the headmaster at the Temple school when all the other teachers died. After the Temple fell, he became a slave to a man who later became my uncle. My father met my mother when she came to Jerusalem to atone at the Temple, but she could not enter through the city gates because the Romans had blockaded the city. She found an ancient tunnel and entered the Holy City from below. My dad was the first person she met when she entered. After the Temple fell, they met at a house much like this one, and they were filled with the Holy Spirit. They were both excellent students, and Luke asked them both to transcribe and make copies of his words. Uncle Rufus had those copies safely delivered to synagogues across the empire. They started a school not far from here and taught others how Yeshua fulfilled the sacred scrolls of Isaiah and others," he said.

"I am in awe. Yael and Benji told me of this female rabbi; I did not know that she was your mother," he said. Caleb pulled out the hot bread from the oven, broke it, and gave thanks. Caleb offered Zev the first choice of food and refrained from eating until Zev had already consumed the first three bites, per Hebrew custom. Once Caleb started eating, Zev returned to sharing his words for Caleb.

"I am here because I let the bad events of my life stall my walk with everyone, included Yahweh. You have already lived a lifetime, yet more of your life remains in front of you than behind you. My wife is gone, and Yael is now my only child with her that remains. Yet, you have done a better job at protecting her than I ever have. Here, take this. You will know what to do with it when it is the right time," he said. Zev reached into his coin pouch on his inner cloak and took out a small piece of silk. Inside of it was a small ring.

"I gave this to my wife many years ago when I committed to her. Since you are willing to die for my daughter, this is the natural next step for both of you. You have my permission to enter into erusin with my daughter."

"What do you want me to do with this?" Caleb rhetorically asked.

"When the time is right, give it to her. Tell her you already have my blessings."

Caleb was at a loss for words. He had taken to heart Dor's reprimand about holding hands with any woman until he was ready to commit. Deep down, he had since concluded that one day, it would be Yael, but he did not think it would be anytime soon.

"Uncle, I am not ready. Yes, she is dear to me, and I greatly desire her, but I chose to comply with the rabbi's requests to refrain from anything our culture says is inappropriate before marriage. But being with her and near her brings me great happiness. I have not yet had a bar mitzvah, so I cannot marry her," said Caleb, expressing a sense of disbelief that this man could suggest marrying his daughter. Normally the boy's family engages the daughter's family. However, Caleb's lack of parents meant that both of them explore an alternative way of negotiating this event.

"This act will make you my son-in-law, and you are first required to build a home for her to live in. I do not know where you will choose to settle, as your life remains in tatters. It is my promise to you that wherever you settle, I will come and help you build."

Zev did not wait for another objection but instead continued.

"And yes, I already spoke to Benji about this, and he approves," he said. Zev could already tell that Benji was a surrogate father for Caleb now.

"You already love my daughter. She has long since fallen in love with you. You need to be the leader of your future household and talk to her about this. You will enrich her heart when you do so," he said.

Meanwhile, two of the kitchen staff had come downstairs and entered the kitchen. They walked barefoot, as they were instructed not to make noise during the night as they moved about the house.

"Gentlemen, if you will accept, we offer to help you with this beautiful project," they said.

Moments later, the entire loaf of bread was eaten, and a plan was discussed and set.

The baker put his arm on Caleb and spoke.

"When it was time for my erusin, my parents selected for me a beautiful girl from a village next to ours. I knew her from the many celebrations we had together, but I was not ready to marry her. I had no idea what I was going to do. I knew it would take a year or more to build our first home, and by then, I would be more than ready. But for me, the magic did not come from the anticipation of being with her. Committing to her created a new and good reason to get up and live each day. I was not chasing something. I was chasing someone. That, my dear Caleb, is what a man gets from erusin. Look what happened? I have more land and more livestock than a man deserves. None of that can happen without a good woman. Start with her, not with the idea that you need to know what you are doing first," he shared. Caleb nodded as the man slapped him on the back.

"Remember, we already know that you have tasted the joy of holding Yael's hand, as we know how you looked and behaved when you did it. You cannot convince us otherwise, young man. The good news is that we have something we would like to give you to make your erusin even more special," they said, holding back a chuckle as they lightly struck him on his back again.

From that, yet another plan emerged to make things better.

Caleb took the ring and stared into the wall. He never heard Zev walk away and return to bed. The two volunteers also left while Caleb remained in a state of contemplation, unaware that everyone else had left. He put the ring in his pocket and went back to the bedroom. Zev was already asleep and snoring.

Zev was finally getting rest.

OF THOSE WHO SEEK: THE FINAL NIGHT'S CEREMONY

Over the remaining days, all of them continued to have the luxury of being the only residents at the House of Healing, and they all received first-class treatment without the interruptions of arrivals and departures. Both Benji and Dor were able to spend quality time with them. The guests each received half a day of counseling every day, and they all had assignments that required they move about the city and even outside of it to make ready for what Dor and Benji called the graduation night.

As a final act of healing, each of them was given a charge to publicly display how they would accept their new self and new identities. During the final evening, they would put their efforts on display and receive prayer. They all needed to vet their plans with a rabbi beforehand to get his guidance and blessings.

As the night came and the sun began to set, new people arrived at the house. All of the women from Golan Heights were preparing to depart, and the next group had come. The housekeepers decided to stay an extra night, as they wanted to see this ceremony. The men from Gaza were prepared to leave the night before as well, but they all decided to stay to participate in the event. All the while, their head of groundskeeping had arrived, and this would be their first experience in the house.

Both rabbis stood at the fireplace with all the chairs arranged around it so that whoever stood by the fire could be seen by all. Everyone had eaten a wonderful early dinner, and the cleanup was complete. As everyone took seats by the fireplace, large pots of chamomile tea were set on each side of the room for anyone to partake when the feeling came upon them. Benji and Dor stepped forward.

"Tonight, we celebrate your graduation ceremony. That does not mean that healing is complete: it means that all the healing we can help with has commenced. As everyone leaves here, we pray that you take away what you have learned and do two things with it. First, we expect you to treat yourself as Yeshua treats you and be kind to yourself as you come to peace with your new identities that are part of experiencing trauma. Second, we expect that you share what you have learned with others who come into your lives. The impact of this place was not given to you and meant to stop with you. It is meant to pass through you. This is what it means to follow Yeshua."

Benji looked around to make eye contact with everyone in attendance.

"The psalmist King David wrote this: 'You keep track of all my wanderings. My tears are on your scroll. Are they not recorded in your book?'[5] Tonight, each of our guests will share their wanderings and present to us their offering to our great Jehovah Jireh as a response to their hearts. For His part, Yeshua will write them in His book, as is promised."

Dor then took over the conversation.

"Tonight, I tell you the truth. History will change. Lift up Yahweh as your witness it," he said.

The first person to come up was Zev. Zev stood before everyone, obviously nervous due to his lack of experience as a public speaker.

"My great sorrow is my failure to love as I have been loved. I failed to see how blessed I have been. I have failed to see how much good I have been able to do, as my sorrows from my loss have been great."

He pulled a small leather pouch from his cloak and held it in his hands.

"Tonight, I wish to make it right with those whom I have rejected who are dearest to me as well as those who wish to be. Tonight, before you all, I wish to confront these lies that I am not worthy of love and acceptance and tell the enemy and tell you the truth," he said.

All of the men from Gaza clapped, and the women from the Golan Heights looked at the men from Gaza in an almost embarrassed way.

"I have been fortunate to have a wonderful woman in my life that I bore three children with. One of those children, my daughter Yael, is with us tonight," he said. More applause came from the Gaza guys.

"I have also been a participant in my community and helped our village thrive for many years. For this, I am proud! However, I have poorly treated Yael. Yet, she chooses to embrace me and love me for who I am."

"Tonight, as my restoration act, I wish to make an atoning offer that transcends all that I love. I decided several days ago to take my wife's jewelry and melt them down to make something special. It is made from all that remains from the most special person in my life. Yael, come forward and receive this gift from your mother and me," he said.

Yael looked at Eliza and stood to walk to her father. When she reached him, he kissed her three times, as is Hebrew tradition, and he spoke a prayer to Yahweh, thanking Him for the blessings of having a daughter.

"I took your mother's necklace and her bangles and had them melted down to make this for you," he said. He removed part of the contents of the leather pouch in his hands. He lifted a perfect silver necklace made with pearls and rubies and placed it around her neck. The sparkle and the colors were pronounced on the other side of the room, despite the poor lighting the fireplace provided. It was an artifact of immeasurable worth.

"The pearls and precious stones came from the men from Gaza who have been cooking and serving us these last four days. They also think you are a beautiful daughter and wanted to help. They knew that you deserved this and made sure that this jewelry was completed before this evening," he said. Yael covered her face, turned to the men, and bowed as an act of reverence and gratitude.

"I am pleased with you, my daughter. You make me proud, and I bless you with all my being. I bless your ways and your choices. I also think you are not done with your seeking and your adventures. Take this with you, to know that I am with you as you go through life," he said, and he kissed her three times again.

"Lastly, I wish for my daughter Eliza to come forward, also. Please stand next to your sister," he said. All in the room except the rabbis gasped as Eliza stood and walked forward. She held her head high; this was her dream moment.

"I must start this moment with a confession. I could not embrace your acceptance of me; I believed a lie that I was not worthy of another daughter. The healers here have shown me not only that I was wrong but that Yahweh Himself wanted you to come to me. I give you a necklace identical to the one your sister now wears."

His voice cracked as he lifted a second necklace from his leather pouch and walked behind her to wrap and fasten it on her neck. He then kissed her and walked around her to stand and face her.

"This is but a small token of my acceptance of you as my own."

He adjusted the necklace to make sure that the rubies and pearls were directly over her heart. He looked up at her and made eye contact, allowing her to watch him cry. This represented the most intimate act any man can have with his daughter, for he exposes his heart to her in the most open manner of Hebrew faith. He leaned over and kissed her three times. He then pulled her in for a father-to-daughter embrace. Tears poured from Eliza's eyes, and Yael cried for her sister. Within two breaths, there was not even one dry eye in the room. After a pause, Zev continued, "Much of the material came from the men from Gaza, as I did not have enough precious metal to make both necklaces. When I told them my plan, they pleaded with me to make necklaces large enough and appropriate enough for young women of your character. I resisted them, but as I see both on you wearing them now, I am glad I listened to them."

"You are both precious to me," he said.

"Alas, I am most sure that you, Eliza, are also not done with your adventures," he added, but he began laughing before he finished. With that, both of the rabbis also started to laugh, and within moments, all of them were laughing.

"I commit to refer to you always as my daughter, and I will proudly defend you as my own," Zev said. He made eye contact with Caleb during the exchange. "However, if a sword is required, I will ask Caleb to help," he said, causing everyone to laugh.

"Thank you, Father," both of the girls said. He repeated the act of kissing each girl three times. Yael reached over and held her sister's hand as everyone applauded this union.

Zev placed a chair between his daughters and sat in it.

"Come, my daughters, sit and receive your father's blessings, as have all Hebrew offspring who have come before you," he said. Each girl sat down, one of each side of him, and they placed their hands under his upper legs as was their custom dating back to Isaac and Jacob. All the men in the room accepted their responsibility in the ritual of passing forward family blessings. All of them stepped forward and laid hands on Zev or on a man whose hands were touching Zev. All the women laid their hands on Eliza or Yael, and Zev spoke a prayer that Dor had helped him compose.

"Great Yahweh, You have blessed me with two wonderful daughters. I ask that all the blessings of Yeshua, both in the present and the future, be poured down upon them and that these women be of Your heart and of Your mind. Continue Your work of healing them from their pasts. As is my obligation and my honor, I bless them with all that I am, from the depth of my soul. Give them great men to be their husbands and gift their wombs with children of honor. Grant them long lives and expand their horizons to bear Your name. Amen."

As everyone stood up, tears were flowing from nearly all who were in attendance. All the women embraced the two girls, kissing them, and one of them poured all of the perfume she purchased earlier that day into their hair as an expression of love.

"Very well done, Uncle," said Dor.

Of Healing and Finding Home

As the moment settled, Dor stood and spoke: "In the same way that Yeshua adopted us into His family, you have seen Zev and Eliza adopt each other into their folds. I tell you that this is true. You have seen a piece of the kingdom of Yahweh here this evening. When our Messiah returns, you will see this event amplified as part of our eternal promises," he said, raising his hands to the heavens.

Once he sat down, Yael stepped forward. She had gone in the back to change, and she was now wearing a pure white cloak and pure white under cloak, with her father's necklace now around her neck. She wore a crown made of silver leaves on her head.

"Oh, I had no idea that the men of Gaza were in the business of giving away silver!" she said, making everyone laugh.

"Yes, they, too, provided the material and workmanship needed to make this crown," she said. "They told me, when I shared with them my idea, that a woman who does worship dance needs a crown in the same way the high priest needs a yarmulke to walk into the Holy of Holies."

No one spoke a word, but the two rabbis looked and each other and nodded in complete approval of her analogy. Yael lifted her cloak so as to not let it drag on the dining room floor, and she moved into the center of the room. Two men came back from the kitchen. One had a flute, the other a drum.

"Before I came to this house, I felt unworthy and dirty. I felt betrayed, and my body was abused many times over the course of a year. When I would look at myself, I would see filth. Since arriving, I see that Yeshua does not see me the way that I do. He sees a beautiful young woman who He wants to see be His child. He wants me to heal. He wants me to forgive everyone from my past, including the Caesar man.

Most of all, He wants me to forgive me," she paused but not to look down, as was Hebrew custom during moments of shame. Instead, she lifted her hands to the heavens and lifted her head as if she were feeling warm rays of sun on her face at first light in the summertime. She opened her mouth and spoke with an authority none had ever heard her use.

"I have learned that Yeshua is a Yahweh of renewal, and tonight, I wish to renew my sacred commitment to sexual purity and return to a spiritual state of purity before Him and before you. Tonight, I will dance unto Yahweh with all my being. And, I do this before you, as witnesses to my commitment. Tonight, I dance for restoration, not because I must, but because I can. I have a choice today. Today, my choice is the love of Yahweh, who sent me the gift that saves us all."

Everyone else joined her with raised hands and raised heads. Benji placed his hand on Zev, and upon his touch, Zev began to weep again.

"I selected these holy words after watching my sister speak with the emperor and allow Yeshua to change his heart. Surely, this was a miracle. These words were originally part of a song that came from David and Bathsheba's fornication. Today, they have a new meaning for me. It is my hope that they have a new meaning for you, too."

The men from Gaza began playing the flute and the small drum as Yael started to dance. She spoke with power and sang the song that was also a prayer: "Create in me a pure heart, Yahweh. Make my spirit right again. Do not send me away from You or take Your Holy Spirit away from me. Give me back the joy of Your salvation. Keep me strong by giving me a willing spirit. Then, I will teach Your ways to those who do wrong, and sinners will turn back to You."[6]

Yael moved about in the center of the room, and everyone watched her. As she circled around, she routinely made eye contact with Caleb, Zev, and Eliza, always raising her hands to heaven. She whirled, allowing the bottom of her gown to create a beautiful but short-lived wheel of white cloth. She became a moving image of what love and forgiveness look like in a fallen world. All the while, the crown of silver upon her head reflected the yellow light of the fireplace, leaving flashes on the wall that lasted for a blink of an eye, just like our time on the earth.

When she finished, no one clapped. Her father stepped forward and embraced her, as did Eliza, and she took a seat next to Eliza, full of tears. Dor was about to stand and speak, but Caleb could not contain himself. Without prompting, Caleb stood up and placed himself in front of the fireplace for all to see. He wore new clothing and had been groomed at the local barber. He was bathed and smelled of perfumes.

"My father and mother were the great public speakers. I want to skip that part and make my point. My message is singularly meant for only one person. I have concluded that I cannot proceed with a life of meaning without her," he said. He reached into his pocket and took out a ring. It was not the same ring that Zev had given him. This one was bigger, and it was encrusted with rubies and had been refined to be purer. He approached Yael and went down to his one knee, as was Hebrew custom.

"Yael, I wish to enter into erusin with you. The metal from this ring came from your father, who took it from your mother's hand when she died. The men from Gaza provided the rubies and the smithing to make sure it was made in time to give to you tonight," he said.

He looked up at her for the first time since he began speaking. Her mouth was open as he spoke.

"I promise to love you in the same way my father loved my mother. I will never see you as defiled or dirty, and I did not need your dance to convince me that Yahweh has made you new. I will honor you, just as my father honored my mother, and I will treat you the way Yeshua treated the synagogue, willing to die for it. Yael, I wish to enter into erusin with you; I publicly commit that I am willing to die for you. Will you accept me as your future husband?" he said.

"Yes, Caleb, I agree to the erusin with you," she said, barely able to get the words out between her tears. After hearing the words he had hoped for, Caleb continued.

"We have many things to sort out between us, as I told you yesterday. I do not know where we will live, but it is not a choice that we need not make today. Your father has promised to help us build our house. The men from Gaza have offered us a plot of land if we live there and help them with others like us. My cousin has agreed to speak to the elders in her village about giving us land in Correae. I personally do not know what we will do. All I need to know is if you will do it with me," he said.

"Yes, Caleb, of course. I, too, request that we do this correctly. You must complete your bar mitzvah before we complete our marriage act. Then, I will complete our erusin and become your wife," she said.

Eliza could wait no longer. She ran to Yael and hugged her with the same passion she hugged Caleb at the end of the gladiator fight.

Dor stood up and spoke to the two of them while everyone listened.

"Caleb, Yael, you do not have permission to embrace the other's body. You each have tasks that you are expected to complete before you may become one flesh. That is what our Hebrew heritage asks of you. Will you agree to these terms?" he said. The two of them looked at each other. Yael spoke first.

"I am not a victim now. I have a choice. I choose to comply with your request, rabbi," she said. Caleb stayed where he was but smiled. "Of course. Anything for her," he said.

"Now we all have silver rings!" Caleb said. With that, everyone laughed.

"And we are out of pearls, rubies, and silver. None of us have anything left," said the landowners. More laughter ensued.

ELIZA'S ATONEMENT

They all drank tea and congratulated the newly engaged couple. Then, Eliza told them that she was ready to share. Benji reminded them that everyone would be leaving the next morning, and this was perhaps the last moment this group would ever be together. Eliza now had a sister, and it gave her a new warmth in her soul. However, she also felt the gravity of this last moment, and it reminded her how empty her relationship with Titus ended. She did not want that to happen again.

When Zev called her forward, she was royalty. She felt she heard the sound of a unique trumpet when Zev displayed to her the same affection that he showed Yael. He called her daughter in front of everyone. There is no higher honor within a Hebrew family than to be publicly recognized as family and see the tears of your father. She was forever changed that day, and it was for the better.

Nonetheless, it was her turn to humble herself before everyone. She took her place in front and spoke. She had significant secrets that have haunted her, and now was the time to dispel some of their power.

"Even though I waited to the end to share my part of our ceremony, I remain uncertain. Indeed, it is being afraid that is my shortcoming. I am afraid when I can see the dangers in front of me. I am also afraid when I cannot see my enemy."

She gathered herself in the last of the fire's glow for the evening and continued.

"I have learned it is that which we hid in secret that we are most afraid of. For my activity this evening, I wish to outline all but one of my secret fears. Alas, one of them must remain hidden, as it protects others, and they explicitly told me that I cannot tell of it. This grieves me," she paused to wipe away a tear that she would be required to continue to share with no one.

"I am afraid of being told 'no,'" she started. A few of the women smiled and let for a single laugh when she said it. Once they saw that she was both fragile and serious, they apologized, and Eliza continued.

"Because of this fear, I left Tamar and traveled home by myself without asking permission. Had I asked, my auntie would have told me that I cannot go, so I decided not to ask and simply leave. Before you now, I commit to remembering how my parents told me that I could travel to school alone the next time I fear being told no."

She raised her hands to the heavens and spoke under her breath words that she did not understand. All she knew was that the words were not meant to be kept inside. They were a prayer for the time that made no sense.

"I am also afraid of rejection. I knew it to be the right thing to treat Zev as my father, but I greatly feared him rejecting me."

She reached down and adjusted her new necklace. As she centered it, her voice began to crack as she continued, "As you all can see, he did not reject me," she said as smiles of contentment came upon her. "I commit to reaching out to those whom I want to love me and those whom I want to love even when I fear rejection."

Zev stood and ran to her, and he embraced her one more time before returning to his seat. She blew him a kiss as he walked away, using it as an opportunity to wipe her eyes again.

"I also fear physical harm, and I become paralyzed. Caleb has protected me from harm, and he is good at that. Now, he has committed to building a life with Yael, and he will not be able to protect me. I commit to allowing Yeshua to protect me, as He knows my future."

Caleb wanted to say something to her to ease her pain, but he could not. He had nothing to offer her now.

"I am afraid of letting people down. I am a hard negotiator in the marketplace because some of our village elders expect the greatest profit. I push for the best deal not because I wish it. I push for it because they feel let down when I do not. I commit now to being okay with my best effort and not concern myself with proving something to them."

All the men from Gaza could not hide the conviction that struck them in that moment that their lives had been about wealth accumulation. All but the baker began to weep. They prostrated themselves for a moment, taking a bit of Eliza's moment from her. Eliza needed that moment to regain her composure, and she bore no ill will for their interruption. Once they stood up, she continued.

"Lastly, I am afraid of losing Yael and Caleb. It is the way of things for individuals to become husbands and wives. I commit to praying for them and their happiness and trusting Yahweh to provide for me in the same way He provided for my sister. However, though, I will miss them."

Yael tilted her head slightly and smiled at her sister's grace.

"Well done, Little One," said Dor, walking towards her to embrace her.

"You will always be welcome in this place," he said.

"And you will always be welcome in Gaza, Little One," said the men from Gaza.

"Lastly, to you, sister, whatever sense of obligation you feel, consider it nothing. There is no record keeping between sisters."

THE TRIP TO TAMAR

The next morning started as a cool and windy day, but the skies were clear, and the temperature would warm quickly. Today, many of the volunteers and the four receiving healing were scheduled to depart, and final clean-up between shifts was underway throughout the complex. The young adults would be the first to arrive at their destination, as they planned to buy three horses to carry all their wares to get back to Tamar. Caleb expected the need to move quickly as they followed the trail of the slave traders out of Tamar, so horses made sense. Everyone assumed that they would find Eliza's parents, but no one assumed that Katya and Matthew would be okay. Having horses would give them something to ride on as they departed whatever horror they found at home. They would arrive at mid-day, if not before, even if the horses only trotted.

The rabbis walked Eliza and Caleb down to the marketplace early in the morning before the first meal. It was there that they were exposed to Eliza's stash of coin for the first time. She bought the horses and all their needs and then emptied the bag of coins into Dor's hands.

"I got literally all of this from selling several librae of cinnamon in Rome. I coerced the Romans into paying too much for it, and you are the recipient of my good fortune," she said. Truth be told, the horses took only half of her coin, but what she had left would keep the House of Healing operational for another season.

As everyone gathered to pray for the departing, the rabbis had them form a semi-circle, with all the women to the south and the men to the north, per Hebrew tradition. Men were meant to be the leaders of their households and homes, as standing north represented their role as leader and scout.

As the men prepared the last of the provisions, Rabbi Dor took Eliza aside and spoke to her in private. The conversation was brief, and she ran back to Caleb and Yael when it was over. When they asked her what that was about, she only smiled and said that it was "something to think about," and she would say no more.

Once the volunteers had departed, Zev approached the children and called them to him.

"My children, you have made me proud, and you have helped me begin healing. I am grateful. I wish all of you to go on your way, but I have decided that I will stay here. The rabbis have agreed to let me tend their gardens for a season to prepare them for the summer planting. I still have some things that I wish to talk to them about, and I have no reason to go back to Gezer right now."

All the young seekers nodded both at him and each other. The girls kissed him farewell and bid their father goodbye. In a rather poignant moment, Zev looked at Caleb and spoke. That would perhaps be the only time they were sharing this message.

"Caleb, you will never feel it right to call me father, I know that. Yahweh has called you to honor these women, and that is a small price for me to pay to see you create a great opportunity for them. After all, when you took out the sword and forced me to submit to you, our relationship took a permanent direction that neither of us can unwind. For my part, I am grateful for the correction you imposed on me that day, and the rabbis tell me that you have wisdom beyond your years in your choice to withhold your desire to strike me down. I am also full of joy that you have selected my daughter Yael to become your wife. Had her mother been alive, she would have loved how much you are willing to protect and lead her," he said. Everyone could tell that he had practiced what he was saying.

"Yael, my daughter, you have been blessed with a man of Yahweh who will be taking you on many adventures. You will be safe with him. You are the flesh of my blood and most dear to me. Travel safely, Little One. I love you. I will be there for your wedding. I promise," he said. Yael stepped towards her father and kissed him three times.

None of these messages were easy for him to share. He had lived nearly two last years in shame, and he was beginning to pay the consequences of his dishonest view of himself. He reserved the most difficult and perhaps the most important message till the end.

"Daughter Eliza, you have saved me," he said, allowing the tears to flow evenly. It was obvious that he had more to say, but this was all he could muster before his joy overwhelmed him. "Yes, you have saved me," and Eliza kissed him three times, just like Yael. He motioned for them to leave, and it was obvious he needed some time to mourn. The girls climbed onto their horses and began trotting towards Tamar. As they left, Zev fell to his knees and praised Yahweh for His offering of second chances. Zev's life had never been fuller.

MEMORIES OF TAMAR

Tamar was a unique hamlet, even by Hebrew standards. The village's primary economic activity had changed since the Temple was destroyed. For nearly all of its history, this place was farmland. Now, it was a regional center for educating Yeshuaian children. It was originally the only such village in Judah; now, there were many places where a synagogue and the adjacent school taught the story of the Messiah and his time on the earth. Although the village had a steady number of residents for most of its history, the creation of a boarding school changed that dynamic: the number of students who lived and studied during the school season would cause the village population to triple for many months each year.

The village had peacefully existed for many generations of Hebrews, and it bordered a forest, making the task of gathering materials for expansion easy and fast. Marauders seldom visited this place, as the road to the east traveled to Jerusalem, and the road to the west ended at the coast. No wandering thieves would be able to escape without easily being followed.

The village's leadership made sure that they had all they needed for self-sufficiency during this time of the Roman occupation. Despite its small size, there was a village blacksmith, a grinding mill, shared food storage, nearby hunting grounds, multiple water sources, and ample traffic to support several shops that sold food and offered lodging to traveling merchants. Even without the school, the village would have thrived.

Before the Temple fell, many of the residents worked seasonally in Jerusalem, sending home coin and remittances to their families. Mishi's family was one such group. During the off-seasons, they would cultivate their fields and invest in laborers to perform the harvest and storage, as the lands were rich and fertile. That dynamic changed once the Temple fell. With no work to be found like that in Jerusalem, Caleb's grandparents returned home, and with the help of other families, organized and built a school and a synagogue. Their village had never had a synagogue, and it was their family's promise to start one. Since Mishi was the headmaster at the Temple school before its destruction, there was a great demand that he continue the tradition of formal Hebrew education that prepared youth for rabbinical lives, albeit this time far from Jerusalem. There was an immediate demand for his teaching services, too. They only lacked the facilities and the community awareness to have families send their children to Tamar for their education.

Mishi and Yael's mission immediately became more complicated, as members of The Way in and around Jerusalem knew that Yael had become a rabbi in Hebrew tradition, and they wanted their sons and their daughters to study under her tutelage. High priority was placed on building a dorm for the girls to keep them safe and separate from the boys. Yael herself would teach the girls their first lesson on purity each year as she would teach the importance of avoiding fornication before marriage and its impact on the soul of a teenage girl. Little did Eliza know that her aunt's anecdotal story was a true one.

Of Healing and Finding Home

During the first year of operation, the school only offered instruction when it was possible to teach outside. However, Mishi's father enlisted many of his friends from his days working at the temple, and they were able to complete a sixteen-room two-story school and two dorms in only eight months. Telling all the local Hebrew villages about the new facility that accommodated resident boys and girls was made easy through Rufus's connections. He used his influence in the military to have soldiers carry notes written by Mishi and Yael to surrounding villages, letting them know that they were open to accepting students. Many of the recipients of that announcement were present when Mishi and Yael publicly committed to erusin in the weeks after the Temple fell, and they were keenly aware of the skills that this husband-and-wife couple would bring to this new style of education. By the end of the first year, a second schoolhouse and additional dorms were required. By the end of the tenth year, Roman architects came at Rufus's bequest to assist in structural requirements needed to house the students in multi-story dorms and more thoughtful food storage to accommodate feeding 600 students twice a day.

The remaining Pharisees were intrigued by the presence of girls in the boarding school complex. Normally, Hebrew girls would receive nominal education before they would return home and help their family with their businesses; higher education like *beth midrash*[7] and beyond were historically given only to boys. Now, many girls were enrolled in beth midrash, and the number of Jewish girls who could read, write, speak, and translate multiple languages was growing. Eliza was one of many young girls who gravitated towards finance and business, and their uniqueness in the marketplace allowed them to disrupt a historically "men only" workplace. The positive feedback from the communities was overwhelming, and Yael knew that additional women would need to enter into the ministry to support all the girls who found their niche learning what all the boys were. Tamar was changing Hebrew educational history. Dor understood this more than any other male member of the ministry that served their faith.

When they crested the last hill before the village came into view, they stopped their horses and looked down at the valley. It was a much-needed relief to see that most of that tradition remained. Caleb and Eliza had feared that all signs of the school and the synagogue would be destroyed by fire by the time they returned. Luckily, the opposite was true, and most of their school campus remained intact, and repairs had already restored much of what was damaged. Two of the three school buildings were pristine, and both of the dorms remained usable. Part of the roof of the temple was destroyed, as was a portion of the boys' dorm, yet all three of them could see children playing from their vantage point. This simple sight created great joy for Caleb and Eliza, and they smiled and hugged each other.

"That is my village," said Caleb as he looked at Yael with a big smile on his face.

"That is my school down there, and it is open!" said Eliza, as she burst into tears. Another wave of grief came over her, as she knew that her hero would not be there to greet her and speak with her, and the hole in her heart hurt again. The rabbis taught her to let these floods of emotion pass and not try to intercept or stop them. They also taught both Caleb and Yael to patiently wait for these waves to pass. Eliza wanted to run down and look for her aunt and tell her about her great adventure, but she would not be there for her to run to. She was gone, and there was no one to fill that hole. Her tears were bitter. Yael could offer her no reprieve. Caleb sat down and put Eliza in his lap, and he rocked her back and forth, kissing her head. He repeated to her, "I know. I know. That was my mom, too!" Yael could only sit and stare as the two most important people in her life and the architects of the last two months of her life wept bitter tears, wailing out loud like an animal at a slaughter who saw nothing coming. She reached out to both of them, touching them, lifting their grief high to the heavens, looking for a desperate connection with the Messiah.

"Yeshua, in the manner and method that You pleaded with the Father to take the burden from You, please take this burden from my family. Yet, if it is their cross to bear, give me the grace to bear part of it for them. I offer myself to You and to them to use as You see appropriate. I surrender, my Yeshua. I surrender all to You. I am at a loss to proceed without You and without them. Fill the hole in their life, and use me anyway You can so I can help," she spoke with her hands held high.

Soon, the tears stopped, and they each helped the other to their feet.

"Let's go," said Caleb, as they mounted their horses and rode to the entrance to the village. They dismounted and timidly walked into the village. The same nervousness that Yael felt when she returned home was now upon Caleb and Eliza.

"Caleb, I know what you are feeling. Don't overreact to what you see, my love," Yael said.

"You have never called me that before now," he said.

"You have never needed it to hear it before now. It has been there for a while," she said.

IN AND OUT OF TAMAR

Within moments of walking into the village with their horses, the message had been sent to the school and to the village elders that the two lost students had arrived. The village had awaited their return, and nearly everyone greeted them with great joy and praise to Yahweh that they were still alive. As the greetings continued, Caleb and his old neighbors quickly took the horses to the village manger then returned. When they got back, nearly everyone had gathered in the village square. They all wanted to hear their story.

While Caleb was gone to the manger to get food and water for their horses, Eliza had been busy introducing Yael to all of her school friends and teachers as her sister. Yael was instantaneously accepted by the community, and Eliza and Yael were both quick to showcase the others their rings and necklaces. When Caleb finally returned, all the schoolgirls applauded his return, and many of the girls who had known him his entire life complimented his choice of wife.

"She is beautiful, so beautiful. She will bear you beautiful children, I believe," said one of his friends. Her twin brother was one of Caleb's hunting partners, and he had spent a lot of time with her family. Her opinion mattered to him. "Thanks," he said. He wanted to say more, but there was no time.

When a group of Caleb's friends came up from the school, Caleb took out his Roman bow and ceremonial sword that he got from his time in Rome and let them hold it and pass it around. As boys do, he told partial stories of his time away, very much showcasing what he brought home. Their entrance became a show-and-tell session like what they did at the start of a school year after a month away from each other. This time, though, the artifacts on display were worth more than gold. The stories behind their acquisition were the stuff of prose. However, in that moment, they all were teenagers trying to be children in an occupied and oppressed land.

After another short time, four of the rabbis from the school approached Caleb. As they approached, the three young adults came together, and Caleb spoke for them using a partially prepared script that Benji had helped them create before leaving. Etiquette would require that they answer questions as well as have questions answered, but they needed to communicate their expectations as quickly as they could.

"Teachers, greetings to you all! We have been gone a long time, and we have a long story to tell you. For now, we will tell you only what we can, as we cannot stay here. Since we left, we have visited the House of Healing twice, and we have been to Rome. We have participated in some amazing events, and we want to tell all of you of our tales; however, can you first tell us what has happened since the parents and children were taken captive?" Caleb asked.

He was told to expect resistance to his request. When that happened, he was to allow Eliza to speak.

"Young Caleb! We received messages from Dor and Benji that you were going to Rome, but that is all we know. We have prayed for you and sent out word to see if Eliza had returned to Correae. Please tell us what happened. Don't be hasty!" the history teacher and acting headmaster said.

Of Healing and Finding Home

"Teachers, we wish to respect you and will tell you all that you need to know. For now, you need to know that I was embraced as a member of the House of Flavian and am in good standings of that household now. With this status, I also have a decree signed by the emperor that frees my parents from slavery, assuming that this is what happened to them. Please tell us what you know of what happened to those who were being placed on carts when we were here last," Eliza said. With that, she took off her ring and handed it to the rabbis. Once they inspected it and handed it back, she gave them the royal decree, and they read it out loud for all to hear.

"Young Eliza, this is truly amazing. Yes, we do wish to know more. The carts left with the parents and the children. All the children returned on foot the same day they left, and they said that they were abandoned as the remaining soldiers took the cart of parents to the walls of Jerusalem. We have sent no one there, fearing their wrath from all the killings at Caleb's hands."

For the first time since anyone has discussed Caleb's killings, Caleb felt no shame for his deeds. He knew now that it was for the preservation and defense of his family that he initiated those acts. There was no sense of vengeance in his actions, and he stood worthy before man and Yahweh for his actions. For the first time ever, he smiled on this topic.

"I have the power to pardon Caleb's action, and the emperor himself spoke to me and assured me that the army would comply with my requests," Eliza said. As instructed, she cast her gaze at different adults in the crowd that was gathered.

"What can we do to help you?" said the headmaster.

"Pray," said Yael. There was no script here. Yael instead spoke from her heart.

"We all know we are about to face more uncertainty and more risk as we travel to the walls of Jerusalem, surrounded by Roman authority. We have Caleb's ring and Eliza's ring, and they can help us. However, we want all of our steps to be covered in prayer," she said.

"This is wise. Can I ask what your name is?" the eldest rabbi inquired.

"She is my erusin. She is named Yael, as my mother was," said Caleb, with power in his voice. In the depths of his soul, he wanted to reach over and take her hand, showing the world that she was his and he would kill anyone who crossed her. Yet, he made a promise to do what Yael asked, and Yael herself promised to live pure until her erusin was complete and they were married.

"I had a dream that Yael returned to us. Indeed, the dream happened last night as I slept. I could not recognize the Yael in my dream as she was dressed in all white, dancing before the throne of God, and angels watched her and lifted her up in prayer. She was being made new and would be sent to us," said a different rabbi. Eliza turned toward her sister, and her eyes were wide open. They held hands and smiled. They released their embrace and turned back to the rabbis.

"That was her, not my aunt that you saw, rabbi!" pointing towards Caleb's future wife.

Caleb nodded his head.

"Yes. That was this Yael that you saw, not my mother," he said.

"It is indeed amazing to see how Yeshua works great miracles that we could not have perceived," the rabbi responded.

"Wow," was all that Yael could muster the courage to say. She wanted to diffuse all this talk of a dream and get on the road to find Eliza's parents.

Eliza had already told her girlfriends what she needed, and they came back with bread, fruit, her royal robes from her time in Jerusalem, and two warm scarves.

"Take our gear from our horses and place it in my family's house, in my parent's old bedroom," said Caleb, pointing towards his friends, nodding to them to be quick. They brought back their horses from the manger and emptied their gear as instructed.

"I forgot to give my father his Egyptian towels," said Yael.

"Don't worry. We will be seeing him again, pretty soon, I think," Caleb said.

He quickly entered his house and inventoried their gear. They assumed a fast trip to Jerusalem, arriving late this very afternoon, and sometime in the walled city next to it or camping on the fields in front of Jerusalem, as that was where they intended to begin their search. He took with him only what he needed for that task. They stepped back outside, and the three of them mounted their horses.

Eliza sat on her horse and moved the beast towards the edge of the village square to speak underneath the largest tree. She spoke with volume to ensure all heard her.

"Our people have a great history of overcoming adversity. Thank all of you for your prayer. It is my prayer that we return immediately with my family. I ask you, make that your prayer, too. We are leaving now for Jerusalem. Pray that we find them and return this very day."

With that request, she turned her horse and began traveling in the direction of Jerusalem.

They would not stop again until the city of David was within their sight.

UNEXPECTED RELEASE

Katya was experiencing morning sickness, but she did her best to hide it from the administrator and Roman soldiers, for she had heard many horrific tales as to how pregnant slaves were disposed of if they could not do their job. The other women in the kitchen helped cover for her, distracting the patrols from the space that she worked when she had an upset stomach. She would relieve herself in the chamber pots when no one was looking. If she did have to vomit, other women would act as if they were upset, as well, to make it seem like it was the food that caused the sickness.

She could not have been given a better assignment based on her condition. Working in the kitchen meant that Katya was able to pick and choose what she ate more than nearly any field slave, as she was fueling a growing baby. As she neared the end of her second month of pregnancy, she knew it would only be a matter of time before it would begin to show, and all of her prayers were for the protection of the unborn child and Eliza.

"Yeshua, please send down the Holy Spirit to protect my children. Protect the one that I have been carrying and the one that is out in the wilderness. Guide them both through these uncertain times, and make them strong, like my little sister was strong," she would say. Her prayers for her children often carried her through the day.

Matthew was also equally blessed with a good assignment. He literally never received a reprimand for poor work. He was never struck by any of the foremen. He knew how to sense the level of work effort the men expected, and he made sure to match it and get those around him to do the same. He had two foremen that he worked under, and they both had clear and easy-to-understand intentions. In some instances, the foremen would give him the directions for the day, and they would leave him in charge of the group of eight men to finish what was asked of them. If there was such a thing as an assistant foreman, Matthew was it. All of Matthew's wounds from their capture were healed, and he felt strong.

Matthew greatly benefitted from the extra portion of food that Katya brought home from the kitchens. Most of the men around him slimmed up as the energy they spent moving brick and rubble at the end of winter was less than the energy they consumed. Katya would often bring home a clay pot of extra broth or sometimes even extra goulash that the soldiers did not eat, and he would eat his fill. Matthew's weight remained steady during those first two months, and Katya saw her husband's muscular definition increase.

Their time was not perfect, though. They were slaves, after all. Neither of them had adequate warm weather clothing for life and work outside of Jerusalem. In the evenings, they would huddle underneath the single blanket provided them by the administrator, and they would place both of their outdoor cloaks on top of the blanket to keep warm. Their tent walls protected them from the wind and occasional snow, but they did nothing to protect them from the biting cold in the mornings when Katya would have to get up and go to work before Matthew. Matthew always gave her his outer cloak, and he would take it from her once he came to the breakfast hall. By then, she would have warmed up.

Of Healing and Finding Home

Part of their love tradition carried with them into slavery. Her shift in the kitchens required that she be at work first. As she would leave, he would get up and speak to her, as he knew his wife. She needed endearment as much as she needed warmth.

"My bride, take my cloak again. This is to keep both of you warm. I will see you at sunrise. While you are gone, I will dream about you, and it will make me smile," he would say. He would then kiss her and touch her head. As she would turn and step out of their tent, she would look back and speak to him what her soul could allow.

"You are a good man, Matthew. I am blessed to have you."

One evening at the end of the second month of enslavement, Matthew approached the kitchen to eat dinner. Two soldiers who worked for the administrator came to him. Fear seized him as he was told to stop to listen to them.

"Are you Matthew of Correae?" they asked.

"I am," he said.

"You and your wife are to come with me to see the administrator," they said.

"What is this about?" he asked. He quickly realized that this was inappropriate behavior, and he turned to walk directly into the kitchen to get his wife. The soldiers followed him into the kitchen, and all the kitchen staff watched what was happening. All of them froze, and one of the soldiers yelled at them to return to work. When Matthew reached his wife, she could sense the anxiety in him as well as see the fear on his face.

"Katya, we are to go with these men to see the administrator," he said.

The women in the kitchen watched the event, and they panicked for her. They had seen the soldiers round up slaves like a sheepdog rounds up farm animals, and stories of what happens when slaves are individually isolated seldom had a good ending. One of the other kitchen slaves ran to Katya and hugged her goodbye, but as she did so, she was struck by one of the soldiers with his hand, and she quickly pulled away.

As they approached the camp leader's tent, Katya's heart raced. The tent doors were drawn closed, but she knew the voice that was behind the curtains. She lifted the cloak that she wore when she worked and ran towards the entrance to the administrator's tent. Outside of it stood three horses. She opened the green canvas tent doors and saw her daughter and two others standing next to the administrator. The administrator was holding a piece of ornate paper.

"Eliza, my daughter!" she said.

The administrator rose and placed his hand across his chest, making a fist showing compliance with a direct order.

"By decree of the emperor, Matthew and Katya of Correae, you are hereby released from your term of service to the empire. You are free to go," he stepped out from around his desk and handed Matthew a different folded and sealed document.

"Per our agreement, attached is a document that absolves you from paying any taxes for one year," he said.

Only Matthew heard the administrator speak. Eliza and her mother were already deeply embracing and sobbing. Yael was standing next to Eliza, with a hand on both the women. Caleb and Matthew embraced as well, but since neither was a man of many words, their talk was short and much lower in volume than the girls'.

The administrator allowed a moment of greeting as he held his helmet under his arm, as is Roman custom when receiving an order directly from the emperor. He instructed the two escorts to remove the shackles on their ankles while everyone spoke.

"Mother, I wish to introduce you to someone very dear to me. This is Yael, and she is my sister!" she said. Katya could not comprehend what she just heard, but she embraced Yael, kissing her just as she did her own daughter. Seeing his future wife already accepted by his aunt filled Caleb's heart. All of the three remaining women in his life were now connected. He had secretly hoped that the act of reciprocating daughterhood would be easier with his aunt and uncle than with Zev.

While the girls continued their talk, Caleb looked at Matthew and spoke.

"Uncle, Yael is my erusin," he said.

"I can see that, young man," he said. He placed his hands on his hips and nodded, all the whiling smiling at Caleb.

"Very well done, nephew," he said.

The administrator decided that they had greeted enough, and he needed to proceed with other events.

"You may not return to speak to the other slaves, nor may you get anything from your tent. If there is something you need, please tell my men, and they will retrieve it for you."

Matthew answered for both he and his wife.

"There is nothing that we need," he said.

"Very well, please depart this camp immediately. Speak to no one as you leave," said the administrator. The conversation immediately stopped, and they all stepped outside of the tent.

Caleb took charge of the moment. The full moon was now high enough in the sky to be a source of navigation.

"Auntie and Uncle, I have brought horses with us with the purpose of taking you home to Tamar tonight. Can you make the journey on horseback? We have plenty of moonlight to guide us, and the three of us are rested."

Katya turned to Matthew, full of anxiety, but her spirits were restored, and she was ready to leave this place. It was now time to make the announcement.

"Eliza, Caleb, there is something you need to know. Your mother is with child, and she is sometimes sick in the mornings," Matthew said.

"Mother! How can this be?" said Eliza.

"Your father and I have never been closer in our entire lives. Our faithfulness was rewarded," Katya replied.

Despite the stereotypes associated with all Roman military leadership, the men underneath their uniforms had hearts. The administrator was fond of some of the Hebrew slaves. His superiors demanded success, and he could not openly express this without risk to his family. However, in this moment, the disguise that he wore associated with this role as rigid disciplinarian and project manager now came down. With Katya and Matthew preparing to leave, he decided it was safe to show his unspoken affection for them.

"I already knew that you were with child," said the administrator. He broke his gaze and looked down into the dust at his feet, cracking a partial laugh of joy.

"In fact, had your daughter not arrived with a message from the emperor himself, I was prepared to let you return to your home," he said.

"Good man," said Caleb, breaking eye contact and looking at the two soldiers, nodding his head in affirmation. They both smiled but did not speak in return. The administrator already knew that Caleb wore the ring of a legate and had nothing to prove. He had no reason to restrain his words, either.

"Mother, can you travel?" Eliza asked.

Of Healing and Finding Home

"Yes, dear, I can. Let's go now, please. Matthew?" she broke eye contact with her daughter and looked at her husband for approval. He remained the head of their household. Matthew had already decided that Katya could have whatever she wanted. After all, both of their prayers had just been answered.

"I brought you both some warmer clothing," said Caleb. He opened the leather saddlebag on his horse and took out the two warmer cloaks that Eliza and Yael got from Titus. He also handed his aunt a warm scarf, and he handed the other one to Yael.

"Sorry, Eliza, I only have two of them," he said, realizing that he did not have a scarf for each woman.

"Bless you, my nephew," said Katya as she wrapped the scarf around her neck. Matthew took off her older and tattered cloak and replaced it with the thicker Roman garment. Both Matthew and the administrator stared at the gold thread embroidered into the fabric and the royal purple trim.

"Mother, that is the cloak I got when I was in Rome," Eliza said. This was not the time to talk about meeting the emperor or how she was able to get them set free. For now, Katya looked up at her daughter with eyes of wonder. The administrator spoke up, this time smiling with his hands on his hips again. He had put his helmet down now that he was no longer executing orders of the emperor.

"This is something I have never seen. A slave woman becomes royalty of Rome between the end of the workday and the evening meal. I tell you, we are witnessing—" and with that last word, Eliza cut him off.

"The power of prayer. That is what you meant to say. You are witnessing the power of prayer."

Caleb looked up at her, as did Matthew. Both had a look of fear on their faces. Cutting off a Roman officer or administrator was a punishable offense. At the least, Eliza should have received four lashings. Depending on what she said in response, she could be killed.

The administrator did not respond; she was, after all, a member of the ruling house of the empire. He could not do anything. "Whatever you say," he said.

They got on their horses and traveled down the valley away from Jerusalem. The nearby small city was about to close its gates for the evening when Caleb stopped them.

"Let's stop and eat. Matthew, you have worked all day and need some food in you to stay upright on this horse," he said.

"No, but I am very hungry, as is your aunt," he said. Matthew broke bread and passed it around for everyone. Once the two elders had taken three bites, the children began their meal. With that, they traveled through the night and arrived back at Tamar as the moon prepared to set. Caleb rode on a horse by himself. Yael rode with Eliza, and Matthew rode with Katya. After a few small stream crossings, they reached Tamar at what Caleb thought to be midnight.

Caleb immediately went to the mayor's house and woke him up. He let him know that everyone was back and safe and that they would be sleeping extra tomorrow morning. He also told the mayor that his aunt was pregnant.

Caleb watched everyone walk into the house. Once they were in, he took two of the horses and went towards the stables. He thought that they might be returning in the middle of the night, so he laid out the hay and water for the animals before they departed.

"Caleb, wait," he heard Yael say. He turned and saw that she had also left and had the other horse with her.

"I have the other horse," she said.

"Oh, okay. Bring it with you and follow me," he said as if he were talking to a farm boy.

Caleb quickly set the horses free in the manger and waited to make sure that they found the hay and water he set out for them. After all, it was dark. Once he saw the animals eating, he turned to return to his childhood home.

"Caleb, wait! I wanted to talk to you. You have been very quiet this whole way back. What is wrong? If I am to be your wife, the rabbis said that I need to speak to you when you do not wish to speak."

That last sentence hit him as perhaps one of the most credible comments she had ever made.

"Yes, you are right," he said. He took a couple of breaths and looked down on the ground as they stood at the exit of the manger.

"I have been thinking about what to do next in life. I have an idea. It is crazier than my idea of going to Rome. You really want to hear it, now?" he said.

"What else do we have to do? Eliza and her mom are exhausted, and your uncle needs sleep. I want to be here for you," she said.

"My searching is not done. I have two trips that I want to make. I want to travel to Caesarea and meet Uncle Rufus's dad. This ring is his son's ring, and I want him to know what his son did and how he taught me. I also think he can help me answer some of my questions about life."

He paused, waiting for her to acknowledge what he said.

"Then, I want to travel to Gaul and meet with Ronan's parents and let them know that their son fought alongside me while trying to give them some coin to have a great celebration. I told him I would do that one day before we went into battle, and I have to honor that request," he said.

He paused again. Yael knew this was the start of some intimate thoughts.

"I was going to ask Eliza for her coin to give to Ronan's parents," he said. "Do you think she will say yes? You know her at least as well as I do, now."

Both of them chuckled.

"Well, she loves her coin, that part is true. I think she loves you more, though. If you would like, I can also speak to her," offered Yael.

"No, let's not do it that way. You are now my erusin, and I am yours. Let's talk to her together," he said.

Yael wanted to embrace this man and thank him for his commitment to their future together. But, she knew the rabbi's warnings to be those of wise counsel.

Caleb sat down on a bale of hay next to the horses where the ducks were sleeping, and Yael joined him. After some small talk about how nice it felt to sit on something other than a horse's back, the fatigue of a long day and the relief of finding his aunt and uncle caught up to him.

"Let's go to sleep," he said.

"Caleb, I have something to talk about, too," she said. She waited for him to ask what. When he did, she took a deep breath before proceeding. She forced herself to look him in the eye.

"What do you think of the idea of you and Eliza completing your bar mitzvah and bat mitzvah here in Tamar, now that we have no pressing issues?" she asked. They looked each other in the eye and laughed. Caleb could see that she wanted the same thing he did.

"Sounds like a plan," he said. Then, Yael spoke with the authority she used earlier in the day. She had been Eliza's helper first. She had become his helper, as well. She had always followed the prompts of others, and she had demonstrated total commitment with the limited resources she had.

"Then, we can complete our erusin and be married. I will travel with you everywhere you want, but let's be husband and wife first," she said.

Caleb leaned his head back and nodded several times before speaking.

"Yael, I had that same thought but was scared to say it."

She held his gaze and reciprocated his intimacy. "You are, too, scared?"

"Yes! I mean, no! Let's complete our erusin without deciding on a final place to call home. My parents got married long before they even started building a home for themselves, so I do not see that as a requirement. Dor and I will have to agree to disagree there," he said.

They both sat there in silence for a few more moments.

"I do not want to go to sleep because I do not want to leave you. But we have got to go to sleep. Do you realize how many stories we are going to have to tell in the morning? My aunt will need to hear it all first. You know, she really hates risk and will probably be appalled at all that we have done," he said. Yael had nothing to add; she just wanted to be with him.

They got up and went into the house. They left their shoes at the threshold to the house, and Yael entered first. Yael found Eliza sound asleep under a pile of blankets next to her mother, and Caleb found Matthew covered in blankets, already snoring. Caleb went to the guest room and took out the same musty blankets that had always been there and laid down.

"Yeshua, I am home, but nothing is the same. The only thing that is the same here is You. Do you want me to build a place like this for Yael and me now, or should I consider these dreams to be from You and continue seeking? I loved the trip to Rome and back, and I want to do more like that. I am going to see my great uncle in Caesarea. I pray that You give him some insight, as I want to get his."

BAR MITZVAH, BAT MITZVAH

The following morning, Caleb got up with intent. He stowed his weapons in the guest room and put away all of his Roman apparel. He put on his traditional Hebrew clothing and went directly to the dorm where the rabbis stayed. He did not think anyone in his house would be stirring until the sun was high in the sky, but there would be a lot of noise outside, and that might wake them all up.

Many of the women were already outside gathering water and preparing cooking fires, and he respectfully bowed to each of them. He would not engage in any of their conversational openings, as he needed to vet a plan with the rabbis.

He arrived at their dorm as the first of them were awakening. Normally, students were not allowed in this area. Caleb decided he needed to override the custom and talk to them. Over the last few months, he had seen enough cultural breaches to last a lifetime, and the one learned from his time in Rome was that when a boundary is crossed, it can be uncrossed later. He took off his sandals and entered their kitchen.

"Master Caleb, good to see you this early in the morning. We remain saddened at the loss of your parents and our leaders at the school. What is that we can do for you?"

"How much longer until everyone is here?" he asked. With that, three other rabbis entered the kitchen, as well as two of the slaves who worked at the school.

"I need to speak to you without interruption. I do not think I can do that any other time today except for now. Can we do that?" Caleb asked.

The lead rabbi told one of the slaves to go to the market and buy breakfast and not waste time preparing it. He told the other one to make bottomless cups of tea for everyone. While he prepared the water, Caleb began on his tales.

"Teachers, I cannot believe that I am already back here. I have many stories to tell you, and I feel that I should tell them to every student here," he said.

"We got a message early last month from two rabbis from the House of Healing. They told us that you came to them for help to reconcile with the killing you did in the village and you were en route to seek an audience with the emperor. What happened after that is unknown to us."

"The boat we were on ran aground, and we swam to shore on the coast of the province of Calabria. Before the boat ran aground, Eliza was held down by three men who tried to rape her. When I saw them, I killed two of them, pushing the first one into the ocean. Eliza spared one of them, and he later became a Yeshua follower. We reached Rome and saw some horrible things, but the underground synagogues there helped us devise a plan to enter the Colosseum and get an audience with the emperor. I gave him Rufus's ring and reminded Titus of his past with my uncle. I agreed to fight in the gladiator pits in exchange for what I hoped would be freedom for Eliza's parents. I killed two more people. Eliza took the earnings from winning and bought the freedom of the girl sleeping in our house now, Yael. She and I committed to erusin and marriage a couple of days ago. Her surviving father accepted Eliza as his daughter."

He paused. They all listened and were in great awe and did not know how to start asking him questions. He took that as a good sign, and he continued.

"Yesterday evening, we reached the internment camp, and a couple of guards approached us as we looked for the administrator. They took us directly to him, and Eliza gave them this note," he paused and gave the note to the headmaster so he could read the note out loud for all to hear.

"This is an unbelievable story, young Caleb. Had you not shown us this note, I would not believe any of this," they said. They began to speak among themselves, but Caleb brought it all back to his story.

"There is an even bigger point here. Eliza was able to share the message of Yahweh with Titus, and he prayed to accept Him into his heart. My erusin was present during the event," he said. The men stood and began praising Yahweh.

"The emperor gave Eliza a ring giving her membership in the House of Flavian. Now that Domitian is emperor, Eliza remains a member of the emperor of Rome's family."

He took out Eliza's ring and showed it to the headmaster.

"Caleb, why are you really here? This story could wait till later today, and I can see you telling this many times—"

"Eliza and I wish to complete our bar and bat mitzvahs. Then, I wish to complete my erusin to Yael and marry her. That is why I am here. I want your help in organizing a *b'nai mitzvah*[8] for Eliza and me. We would like to do it as soon as we can," he said.

He then sat down, meaning that he was done talking. All the rabbis shook their heads in disbelief.

"Caleb, you know from our tradition that up until the date of the mitzvah, your parents hold responsibility for your actions. Based on your story, you and Eliza have both long since taken ownership of your actions," a rabbi said, causing everyone to laugh. He handed back Eliza's ring during the laughter.

"Normally, the ceremony requires that your father give part of the prayer. Have you thought about how this shall be addressed?" he asked.

"Yes, now that my uncle Matthew is here, he can do that for both Eliza and me," he shared with authority.

"There is another part of the story that is significant. When Eliza was ministering to Titus, he asked her to stay and continue to teach him. He called her rabbi, as well," Caleb said, pausing only for a moment.

"We haven't talked about it in detail, but you should talk to her. I think she wants to become a rabbi like my mom did," he added.

The room once again became silent.

"Many of us in here knew this. Your mother brought this up at a management committee meeting as well, as she saw the comfort Eliza has when she shares part of the Messiah's message. We need to talk to Eliza," they said.

Caleb went back to the house, and, as expected, there was a crowd of students outside their home, waiting to see and talk to Caleb and Eliza. They were not expecting Caleb to approach them from behind. Many tried to stop and talk to him, but he excused himself and entered the house.

"Good morning, cousin," said Eliza. She was already heating water, and Yael was making fresh bread using some of the oil from Correae that Eliza brought here two months ago.

"Here," he said, handing her back her ring.

"What did they say?" she asked.

"They didn't say no. They do want to talk to you, though. I will make the tea if you want to go over there right now. There are all in the rabbi-only area. I just walked in," he said.

ELIZA'S THOUGHTS ON SEEKING

When she entered the kitchen, it was obvious that the rabbis were surprised to see Eliza arrive so quickly. The food their slave had ordered had not yet come up from the market, but the tea was ready, and the headmaster offered her a cup of it.

"Come, Little One, sit and talk to us. Caleb told us your story this morning, or at least the part of it that he felt he needed to tell us. Do you also wish to complete your bat mitzvah and pursue a new path?" they asked.

"I was asked by Rabbi Dor to come to follow him and become his disciple," she said.

The room went totally silent. The phrase "come to follow me" was used exclusively when one established rabbi saw something in another apprentice that he wanted to help nurture. When a rabbi calls another, he commits to mentoring the called one for several years until they are ready to become a rabbi. Each of these men had been called, and the headmaster himself had called others. They needed no explanation as to the seriousness of this event. There was no higher honor in all of the Hebrew faith than to be called by a rabbi. The headmaster breathed deeply before responding.

"Boys, when Caleb left, I thought I had heard the greatest story of our lifetimes. Indeed, I was wrong!" and they all laughed.

"Eliza, even your aunt was never called. It was a title given to her by Luke himself. Truly, this is the most extraordinary event in our people's spiritual leadership. Even the ancient scrolls make no provision for women to enter this sort of ministry. Yet, if what we heard was true and you sat next to the emperor as he accepted Yeshua as his Savior, then, I, for one, approve of this calling."

He set his gaze upon the others in the room, looking for someone to either agree or disagree with him. A different teacher spoke up.

"Eliza, I have been your teacher since your family first started sending you here some five years ago. Indeed, I remember the first time you recorded the Greek and Hebrew alphabet. I have watched you speak to groups with comfort, and I have seen you encourage your peers while others ridicule them. I not only will stand with you during your b'nai mitzvah but will personally deliver you to your caller, as is our custom. I welcome you to enter our ranks," he said. Other heads nodded, but no one else had anything to add in the moment, so the headmaster continued.

"Dor is trustworthy and honorable. However, you are not yet of age to make this decision. It is uniquely on your father," he said, but she cut him off. She was getting used to cutting off authority figures now.

"Or until I have completed my bat mitzvah and am of age to decide for myself," she said.

"I see. Yes, you are correct. I have not spoken to you, but the Spirit of Yahweh is obviously on you. I would be a fool to deny you the right to answer Dor of your own volition. How much do you remember of the ceremony?" he asked.

"Well, considering I have helped about ten girls practice as they got ready, I pretty much know all of it," she said. Everyone laughed at both her words and her tone. She was a powerful young woman now, but she was still the same girl they knew from the past who defended herself with an attitude of superiority. She made nearly all of them laugh at some point in their careers with her sass.

"Your confidence has grown since you have traveled to Rome, Little One," said her Greek teacher.

"Yes, teacher, it has. When the Holy Spirit guides me, I fear no one, not even the emperor," she said. They all looked at her, and her countenance was undeniable. Her attitude had turned into a powerful weapon of Yahweh that none of them could ever have predicted.

"Very well. We will do it the day before Sabbath. Come, Little One, we will cover you in prayer in the way that all who have been called are covered," he said.

Eliza went down to her knees and raised her head, as instructed. The men held hands and gathered around her, lifting her to follow Yahweh and all His ways, representing the Hebrew faith for all in the world who come to know her. The prayer was quick, and she stood up afterward.

"Teachers, thank you. I will let Caleb know," she said. Before she got up to leave, she asked a question.

"Rabbis, I am not ready to answer Dor. I would like to take a private walk with each of you between now and the Sabbath to ask you some questions about your service," she said with clarity and respect in her voice.

"Of course. You know our schedule. Come any time after school is over, and we will be glad to answer all of your questions," they said.

She turned around and left.

Now, she needed to tell her mother. She was not about to do this without Yael standing next to her.

TELLING HER MOTHER

The Sabbath was only three days away, and the task of organizing a b'nai mitzvah could take as long as a month in a normal community. A b'nai mitzvah is a concurrent ceremony when both the boy and the girl transition to adults and take full responsibility for all of their acts both before Yahweh and before all other Hebrews. Once complete, their parents are no longer responsible for their actions, and it represents a life transition for all Jews. No matter how rich or poor, all Jews between ages twelve and fourteen make this transition.

These events last a full afternoon. There is always a celebration that happens after such an event, and the family whose child is transitioning prepares a huge community meal. Before the celebration begins, the boy and the girl must walk around the synagogue, reading sections of the sacred scrolls out loud to the community. They also do other things that can include worship dance, teaching to the community, or making their first tithe. They also need to make special clothing for the ceremony as well as invite families in surrounding communities to come and watch.

Because of Tamar school's enrollment, combined with its status as a boarding school, b'nai mitzvahs were as easy to do as preparing bread and hummus for fifty people. The school had created a sequence for the transitioning adult to follow, and both Caleb and Eliza had memorized their sections of the scrolls and had talked through their personal additions to the ceremony.

Both agreed that their royal garb from their time in the Colosseum met all the cultural requirements to be "decked out" in the finest clothing. Yael let her borrow the crown that the men from Gaza made for her, and Eliza put on the outer cloak she wore to the Colosseum. When she put it on, Yael began to laugh uncontrollably, saying, "I tell you the truth. This is surely the most provocative garment ever worn at a b'nai mitzvah."

Eliza covered her mouth as she remembered that her gown revealed much of her chest and had an open seam on the left side that exposed the full length of her leg. Between bits of laughter, she took it off, and the two of them walked to the tailer to get it altered.

"That would have been a disaster to wake up tomorrow and not have noticed that!" she said. Eliza wanted to appear as a Hebrew princess and a girl transitioning to womanhood. She did not want to appear as a prostitute.

Caleb, for his part, had some of his father's old clothing tailored to fit him for the event. He also carried the celebratory sword that he received from the emperor, as he and the rabbis came up with a special scene when he would use it during the ceremony. Lastly, each one carried a purse full of copper coins, and they would throw them to the crowd at two different times.

The evening before the big event, Eliza pulled Yael aside and told her everything. The two of them held hands and walked into Caleb's childhood home, where they all had been staying. There were several other women in the kitchen with her mom. Katya had visited Tamar many times over the years, and these women were catching up.

"Mother, can I talk to you?" she asked.

"Yes, speak," she said. All the other women stopped talking.

"Mother, I need you to hear about one other thing that I have not yet told you about," she said.

"Dear, anything, just tell me."

"Rabbi Dor asked me to come and follow him and become his disciple. He thinks I can be like Auntie," she said.

Her mother looked down at the pot she had been stirring, and she became weak. One of the women in the room came to embrace her.

"Darling, I knew that could happen. Your auntie was not just your hero. She was mine too! She had the courage that I never did, and you learned that from her. Oh, you are so young, but I knew many years ago that you would follow in her footsteps. I did not think you would follow so quickly!" Katya said, pausing to wipe the tears from her eyes.

"What about your studies? What about marriage and children? What about helping me with the newborn?" she continued.

The last phrase stunned Eliza, like when the men tried to rape her on the boat. She had not thought about what it would mean for her mother to raise her newborn alone if she was walking in Dor's footsteps as a rabbi in training. Her mother was over thirty years old, and most of her life was the past. She most certainly would need help.

"Mother, I did not even think about the baby," she said. Grief overtook her, and she began to cry again. Her mother walked over to her and embraced her as her little girl, perhaps for the last time. Eliza would complete mitzvah in a day and a half, and she would never again need her mother's permission.

"Eliza, when we brought you into this world, your father and I took you to your uncle Mishi, and he consecrated you.

He prayed that Yahweh's will come to pass, not our fleshly will. He taught a message to everyone in this village that day that we need to submit not only to the Romans but also to Yahweh's will for our life. Sometimes, Yahweh's way is more difficult to swallow than the Roman way. Now is one such moment for me," Katya said.

After the tears stopped, Eliza's mother held her face and looked her in the eye. "If you wish to do this, you will receive your father's and my blessing," she said.

All that remained was for Eliza to decide if she would follow Dor.

B'NAI MITZVAH

The scripted portion of the b'nai mitzvah went quickly, as neither Caleb nor Eliza made any mistakes that would have required that they begin again. As they neared the altar in the synagogue at the end of their walk, they had exhausted all of their coins. They stepped toward the altar, where they would read from the sacred scrolls, and Caleb spoke first.

"I have brought with me this sword. It was given to me by the emperor himself," he said. He took it out of its scabbard and laid it on the altar. Nearly everyone gasped, as he had not yet made it known to all that the sword came from the emperor.

"I have discovered over these last two months that I am a protector. I battled demons in my head at night as I contemplated what I am to do with this calling. I, like you, am a seeker, trying to find the sacred space where my skills and my heart's callings collide."

"Like my uncle before me, I see that it is my life song to protect others who serve our Yahweh. Today, I lay this blade on the altar for Yahweh's blessing and for yours, as you are all that is left of my family now."

As was part of their script, Yael stepped up on the dais of the altar, taking her place next to Caleb. She wore the white clothing she had when she performed her restorative worship dance. She bowed her head as a sign of respect for the future head of her household. None had seen her in her all-white before, and everyone was in awe at her beauty. She was no longer Caleb's erusin; she was also a majestic woman of Yahweh.

"Once this ceremony is done, I shall travel forth to Caesarea to meet with my great uncle, asking him what I should do for additional training to serve Yahweh's people in this role," he said. Once done, he stepped onto the altar and opened the scrolls. He read a section of Isaiah that applied to them all before he rearranged the paper.

"In honor of my parents, I wish to read a section of the book that they transcribed that was very special to them. When my father finished transcribing this, he and Luke cried bitter tears. Let me now tell you that story.

> Jesus continued: "There was a man who had two sons. The younger one said to his father, 'Father, give me my share of the estate.' So the father divided his property between them. Not long after that, the younger son got together all he had, set off for a distant country and there squandered his wealth in wild living. After he had spent everything, there was a severe famine in that whole country, and he began to be in need. So, he went and hired himself out to a citizen of that country, who sent him to his fields to feed pigs. He longed to fill his stomach with the pods that the pigs were eating, but no one gave him anything. When he came to his senses, he said, 'How many of my father's hired servants have food to spare, and here I am starving to death! I

will set out and go back to my father and say to him, 'Father, I have sinned against heaven and against you. I am no longer worthy to be called your son; make me like one of your hired servants.' So, he got up and went to his father. But while he was still a long way off, his father saw him and was filled with compassion for him; he ran to his son, threw his arms around him and kissed him. The son said to him, 'Father, I have sinned against heaven and against you. I am no longer worthy to be called your son.' But the father said to his servants, 'Quick! Bring the best robe and put it on him. Put a ring on his finger and sandals on his feet. Bring the fattened calf and kill it. Let's have a feast and celebrate. For this son of mine was dead and is alive again; he was lost and is found.' So they began to celebrate. Meanwhile, the older son was in the field. When he came near the house, he heard music and dancing. So he called one of the servants and asked him what was going on. 'Your brother has come,' he replied, 'and your father has killed the fattened calf because he has him back safe and sound.' The older brother became angry and refused to go in. So his father went out and pleaded with him. But he answered his father, 'Look! All these years I've been slaving for you and never disobeyed your orders. Yet you never gave me even a young goat so I could celebrate with my friends. But when this son of yours who has squandered your property with prostitutes comes home, you kill the fattened calf for him!' 'My son,' the father said, 'you are always with me, and everything I have is yours. But we had to celebrate and be glad, because this brother of yours was dead and is alive again; he was lost and is found."[9]

"Although I will never see my parents again until I reach heaven, I will always treasure the meaning of this story. I am a seeker no different than this prodigal son, and I have returned," he said. When he was done, Caleb took the blade, attached it to his belt, and stood in front of the altar like the proud man he had formally become.

"I have spoken," he said, signifying the end of his part of the b'nai mitzvah. He then moved off of the altar area and stepped to the far side.

Before Eliza started her role in the ceremony, her parents stood up and stepped towards the altar but stopped short of the dais. Matthew was the public speaker in their marriage, so he turned and spoke to the crowd.

"Greetings to my family in Tamar. We wish to extend honor today as well and add both to our celebration and our embrace of change that is happening all around us."

He and Katya raised their hands to their chest as a sign of gratitude, and they made eye contact with as many in the crowd as they could. Then, Matthew continued.

"When we saw our daughter for the first time a few days ago, it was an answered prayer for us. We had been enslaved, and she and Caleb had fled for their lives more than two months earlier, and we had only limited hope. We prayed that we would see her again, but we did not know if this would come to pass."

He paused to look at his wife.

"When we saw our little one for the first time in the tent of the administrator, she and my wife embraced. Then, she said, 'Mother, I wish to introduce you to someone very dear to me. This is Yael, and she is my sister!'"

Matthew had practiced this portion of his presentation repeatedly because he did not wish to cry in front of everyone. His practice did not help him, as his voice was cracking, and both he and Katya began to cry. Matthew did not let this derail his moment of investment, and he forced himself to continue.

"Over these last days, we have heard many stories from our children, and we are glad you all get to hear these stories now, without interruption. However, before we witness the end of our daughter's bat mitzvah, we wish to call, whom we now tell you all are, both our daughters to the front of our synagogue," he said.

Neither Eliza nor Yael knew that this was happening, and they wore shock on their face as they stood and walked towards their parents. Both were adorned in the best clothing that they owned, and the moment fit their present circumstance. Matthew and Katya took one step down and faced the crowd, but they placed both Yael and Eliza one step higher than them.

"It is our Hebrew way to see our children outperform and outachieve anything we have done. In this moment, we stand one step below our children not just as a challenge but as a public statement that my bride and I believe that these two women will outdo us."

Eliza put her arm through Yael's and held her upper arm. They both smiled as Matthew continued.

"While Eliza was away in the Colosseum in Rome, she made a connection with another Hebrew girl whose place in her heart was immediate. It represents a mystery that cannot be explained with words. Indeed, it was the very first thing she decided to tell us about her trip to Rome, which is quite unusual for those of you who know her!"

Matthew let the crowd laugh for a moment before continuing.

"Over these last days, it is obvious that Yael is the sister that Eliza never had, although that might change next year when my Katya gives birth!" he said, allowing for another bout of laughter. Then, he continued.

"My wife and I were both touched when we saw what Yael's father gave to his two daughters. We have decided to honor this new tradition of Zev by adding to the memories each of these women wears around their necks."

Matthew paused long enough for Katya to take off the girl's necklaces and add two charms to each one.

"Let me explain the meaning of what we have done so that none may boast. Each of these two charms is made of silver. Both are ornate carvings of homes: one is that of a traditional Hebrew home, and the other is a royal palace. These have two meanings. The first is that each of these sisters has two homes that they can call their own, and we look forward to the day we get to meet Zev. The second is that you have a simple home on the earth, but your real palace that neither of you sees is in heaven with our Savior. Therein lies your real hope of the future. As young seekers, we want you to know the truth of the end result of your wanderings."

It was now Katya's turn to speak. She, too, had practiced.

"Daughters, we want both of you to know that we accept you as equals. You both may call us mother and father.

Both of you, continue to wear these necklaces and know that both sets of parents love you and care for you."

"Eliza?" said Katya, signifying that Eliza was to humble herself and bow her head to receive the necklace with its additional adornments.

"Yael?" she said, repeating the act. Katya looked at each one and kissed them three times each, calling them "daughter" at the end. Finally, Matthew repeated the triple kissing, calling each one of them "daughter" as well. Katya stepped up to the same step that the girls occupied and stood between them. She held one of them in each hand as they made a line in front of the altar but far below it to signify that the altar remained the most important place today.

This next moment was the first time that Katya had ever spoken the words written on the sacred scrolls in the synagogue. However, the pride she felt toward these two empowered her to overcome any hesitancy that typically came with first teaching.

"As we all know, Jacob called his twelve sons to his deathbed and blessed each one of them. We all know that he also had daughters like Dinah, but we do not hear of his daughters receiving his blessings. I have spoken to our leaders, and today we start another new tradition, all in line with what Yahweh revealed to us when he sent his only Son to save us from our sins. Today, I wish to offer blessings to the girls of my family as the matriarch."

Matthew had already gone to get a chair for Katya to sit on, as well as two of the synagogue pillows for his daughters to kneel on.

Katya sat down in the chair and spoke out to the crowd of mostly students.

"Girls, get on your knees and prepare yourselves to receive a mother's blessing. Boys, step to the back of the synagogue and witness this for your family and their family after them." She then looked at each of her daughters and smiled.

At that moment, Katya closed her eyes and lifted her hands to heaven. A powerful sense of gratitude that no words could explain as the last few months of her life began to take on a new meaning. Yahweh was gifting not just with a husband who loved her but young women that she was to mentor and that would replace her one day. She wanted them to be better than her, and she did not fear the cost. Not only were two of them in front of her, but one was inside of her. Not long ago, she thought she had none. Yahweh honored her faithfulness, and she could not contain herself. From the top of her lungs, she spoke and began to sing:

"My daughters, per Hebrew tradition, place your hands under my upper thighs and receive my prayers. These words came from our great forefather Aaron, and he gave them to our people during the times surrounding the Exodus from Egypt."

As the girls positioned their hands under their mother's legs, they bowed their heads in reverence as Katya placed her hand on their heads. She began first with a prayer, then ending with a song that she made for this moment.

"Jehovah Jireh, you have blessed me not only with two beautiful daughters but also with another child in my womb. I have no greater desire than to see this same blessing bestowed on every girl and woman in this room. Yeshua, protect all these women from the evil one. Allow their wombs to bear children. Grant them loving husbands who see the wisdom of having educated women in charge of the household and let them find great joy in helping their husband until his last days. Yahweh, I grant all my blessings to the two with me and the one still inside of me, and I consecrate them for You both on the earth and in eternity. Let them play a role in expanding Your kingdom to bear Your name."

Then, she began swaying to each side as the ancient words took a melodic shape, and the ambiance of a new song came from her lips.

"May Yahweh bless us,
May He keep us,
May He show favor towards us.
May He grant us grace,
May He grant us peace
For a thousand generations.
May He bless us,
All around us
And be with us,
And go with us.
May He dwell within us,
May He bring peace."

She continued singing it, and several other girls stood up and began singing with her. Soon, the mayor of their village stood and joined them, signaling the rest of the village to join. By the end of the third round of signing, everyone in the village joined.

She stood up and took her daughters, one in each hand, standing like a queen before a valley of her most loyal servants and spoke. She allowed everyone a moment to wipe the tears of joy that had filled everyone's eyes before she spoke.

"Ladies and gentlemen, students and teachers, parents and friends, I present to you my two daughters!"

All the joy that she had contained was now free to flow, and the entire synagogue erupted in applause. This time, everyone clapped for joy as Yael was formally welcomed into their community.

As everyone took their seats, Eliza stepped towards the altar, as it was her time.

ELIZA'S MITZVAH

When Eliza reached the end of her readings and storytelling, she stepped to the altar to speak. Even though she lacked a script to follow as her parents had urged her to do, she felt comfortable.

"When I left this village over two months ago, I was scared and felt paralyzed during moments when I needed to move. I experienced some terrible things and saw some awful events, none of which were intended. As I have learned from my time at the House of Healing, these events altered my direction.

"Like my cousin and my aunt before me, I am a seeker. I sought out adventure, not realizing how that adventure might bind me. I was not prepared to experience what I did, and I needed healing.

"My auntie passed away, and that was most difficult for me. She was my hero, and I wanted to be like her. Little did I know my prayer would be heard, and I am at a crossroad no different than the one that Simon and Peter experienced on the shores of the lake when Yeshua called them. They were not ready."

She paused and adjusted her necklace and royal garb.

"I have been called to follow Rabbi Dor and become one of his disciples," she said. This was perhaps the most radical of all the new traditions proposed so far that day. Since only the schoolteachers and her family knew, many gasped and spoke to one another as to what this meant for their faith. She gave them a moment before she continued.

"However, I have decided that family is too important to ignore. Before I accept his calling, I will do two things. I will be with my mother as she delivers my sibling, and I will care for it with her until she is able to do this alone. Second, I will marry, making sure my family selects for me a man who can embrace my calling. Then, I will take the path of my auntie before me and become a rabbi for our faith."

She paused to look around the room.

"I have spoken."

BEFORE THE TRIP
TO CAESAREA

Caleb sent no word to his great uncle Cornelius that he was coming. He anticipated riding two days on horseback, reaching this coastal town late on the second day. The road was well-traveled, and now that he had completed his mitzvah, he did not need anyone's permission.

He felt none of the nerves that normally would accompany meeting a man of high esteem both in the Roman Empire and the Hebrew faith. Caleb knew that he needed some guidance before he could proceed with the rest of his life, and he hoped and prayed that Cornelius would have answers for him. Others in Tamar claimed that Caleb had met Cornelius when he was a young boy, but he had no memories of such an encounter.

Before he left, he spent every free moment with Yael and his aunt and uncle. They had much to do before he could complete the *chuppah*[10] *ceremony with Yael and become man and wife. They required a marriage contract, or ketubah*, as well as signatures from two non-family members who approved of this union. They needed to write invitations and send them to everyone whom they thought should come, as well as make provisions for the wedding feast afterward. For the most part, Caleb did not care. On every detail, Yael and Eliza seemed to talk without end before everyone would reach an agreement.

Yet, Caleb knew that he and Yael had much to discuss before leaving regarding their future together. Caleb would end each day by taking Yael for a walk, and they would talk.

"Yael, after listening to the men on the boats and talking to the two assistants in the yellow door synagogue back in Rome, I am hungrier than ever to explore and discover the remnants of Creation," he said. She listened and walked next to him.

He spent time on those walks with her reiterating his dreams. She often asked him questions about the ideas that came to him; after all, she had only known him for two months. She learned his love language. She learned to say uplifting things as well as point out errors in his thinking.

Caleb was amazed at her insight. He repeatedly would tell her during the day that he wanted her opinion on these issues. That, in turn, validated her. In this way, they were already married.

She learned that he was not open to negotiation with his desire to visit Gaul and find Ronan's family and share with them about their son and their time in the gladiator pits. He also wanted to visit Messina and explore the volcano that captured their attention when they sailed through the strait of Messina last month. He wanted to see the inside of Jerusalem, as well.

She also knew it was his calling to protect, but she told him he needed to find someone else like his uncle to finish what was started in his education. He quickly cast out the idea of returning to Rome to train with the emperor's elite squad, but he did agree that he was missing some things. His next step was a trip to visit his uncle's father.

"Caleb, while you are away getting your questions answered, there is another one that I want you to ponder. Eliza and I both want a family, and this is our calling. It is complicated for me to hear you speak of these dreams and find a place where I, too, can have the desire of my heart. Eliza is called to become a rabbi, and you are called to travel and protect. Once she begins to follow Dor, she has no idea what that will mean nor where it will take her. Neither of us knows what to do with all this uncertainty. With you and me completing erusin and becoming one, I am driven to know some of these answers. I will follow you to the end, but I do not know where we are going. This scares me like Rome does," she shared, perhaps with more passion than any other message she has shared since coming to Tamar.

"Caleb, I need to be safe," she said, "Words cannot express how important this is to me."

Caleb knew this to be true. His uncle had repeatedly told him that women need to feel safe and men need an adventure to be complete. If one spouse did not provide for this outcome for the other spouse, the marriage could not thrive as it was intended. It was the duty of both husband and wife to resolve these issues.

"Okay, I will ponder what you said and perhaps talk to Uncle Cornelius about that," he offered.

After three more nights in Tamar, Caleb decided to depart at first light using the same horse that he used when he traveled to Jerusalem to rescue Matthew and Katya. The weather had changed, and springtime was now upon this part of the world. Although he would be traveling much to the north to reach Caesarea, he would also be on the coast, meaning milder weather and potentially wetter weather. He packed not only all the same things that he packed for Rome, but he took a dried deerskin in case he was caught in a spring rain. For the first trip by himself, this sortie had big expectations.

Caleb lacked a father in the moment, but his aunt and uncle were living with them for a few days. He chose to follow his uncle's example as he went out of his childhood home to get on his horse to leave. However, before he left, he had one more conversation with Yael.

"Yael, I am doing this trip to help prepare for our lives together. I do not know what answers I will find, but I am finding them for you and for us. I will love you this way, all of my days. On my honor, I swear this oath to you. I know it is my responsibility to say this to you at our wedding, and I am supposed to say it first. I love you," he said.

Eliza and her parents watched and heard the exchange. Matthew put his arm around his wife and drew her to him while Eliza turned to look at her parents.

"Dear, he takes after you!" Katya whispered to Matthew, and all three of them laughed.

"And I love you, Caleb," Yael said.

Eliza wanted to run to her sister and embrace her. However, she could only stare to the side and allow a tear to flow. Yael remained her sister, but her sister was now becoming Caleb's wife. The goal of any seeker is the discovery of what lies next in life's path. Part of that answer includes a departure from what was. Caleb represented what was next for Yael. Caleb was now perhaps starting to represent the past for Eliza. Her heart hurt.

QUESTIONS AND ANSWERS IN CAESAREA

Caesarea was one of three important ports that the empire used to bring goods and services in and out of Judah. Caesarea was much bigger than Tamar or Kedron, as it was a port city that was constructed by Herod during the time of Yeshua. Caleb arrived in Caesarea a few days before a large flotilla of troops was scheduled to come from a training post on the island of Crete. It would be the first assignment for nearly every one of these new soldiers, and Cornelius was one of several who were responsible for training them. Most of them would be in a construction role. The architects and engineers had two projects that they wished to accomplish with this group. The wharfs were falling apart and needed to be rebuilt, and there was a growing need for aqueducts to bring fresh water into the city from the inland hills. The first teams completed all the designs and drawings, and they had negotiated trade agreements to provide for ongoing food supplies for the vast number of men who were about to arrive.

The final step to beginning the construction was training the laborers who would do the work, and for this, the Romans nearly always used soldiers. Most of them could not read nor write, but they all were excited about the coin that they would earn for public works duty and a stipend for overseas work. They were always the last to arrive on site. Caleb reached the city during a lull in activity immediately before the harbor became full of ships unloading soldiers and supplies.

Rufus taught him to ask the village blacksmith any questions. He was always easy to find and was often the most honest and dependable source of information. When Caleb arrived, he followed Rufus's advice. He stepped off his horse and walked to the village blacksmith.

"I am looking for my uncle's father, Cornelius the centurion. Where can I find him?"

He was redirected to a large homestead on the southern edge of town. When he arrived at the compound where Cornelius and his family lived, he was approached by an older Jewish man who wore Hebrew clothing and a yarmulke to cover his head.

"Excuse me, sir, I am looking for the father of my uncle, Cornelius. Can you point me to him?"

The old man smiled and looked up. "Hmm? Come, boy, walk with me. I will take you inside his home. Leave your horse here," he said, pointing towards a wooden railing next to the all-brick compound. The old man waited for Caleb to return to the threshold of the home. He had already taken off his shoes and stood looking at him as he approached.

"So, you must be Mishi and Yael's boy, no?" he asked.

"I am," said Caleb. He was at a loss as to how this man knew him.

"Come, let's get you washed up and put something in your stomach. I want the whole story of what happened to my son," he said. Caleb gasped.

This was Cornelius, and he obviously knew something about what happened to his son. Caleb guessed that he would be telling stories before he would be listening to them.

They walked through Cornelius's family mansion, and Caleb was in awe. The first room was his hall of accolades. The first point of interest was his insignia for becoming a tribune. Caleb did not know that he had been promoted above the rank of the centurion and was now one of six men in charge of the tasks associated with keeping a legion of men occupied and engaged in their task. This was a great accomplishment. As Caleb stopped to look at it, Cornelius approached him and spoke.

"I suspect what you are here for it isn't in this room, boy. Let's keep going," he said.

The kitchen was next, and it was uniquely Hebrew. The bowl placement and storage of grain had all been done in the Hebrew way. There were also no slaughtering or meat storage areas within the house, also a Hebrew tradition that came down to them from the writings of the prophets.

Caleb was not about to drop the impact of what he saw in the previous room. "So, Uncle, you are now a tribune?" he said.

"I am. I still do the same thing that I always have done. I mentor people. I lead justice missions. I teach how to have integrity when no one is looking," he said as he stepped into the kitchen to get one of his slaves to pour them two large cups of tea. They walked up two flights of stairs and stepped onto the roof of his home. Cornelius's family had placed several large wicker couches on the rooftop, and there was a hinged box containing blankets and pillows next to the couches. Cornelius took a blanket out and sat on one of the couches. He motioned to one of his slaves to go downstairs and prepare a meal. He made a gesture that meant "go kill a chicken," and the slave left.

"We shall have meat, bread, and cabbage this evening. I promise you will love it," Cornelius said.

Caleb wanted to jump into the reason he was there and tell Cornelius all the stories that he could. After a few words, Cornelius held up his finger, demanding that Caleb wait a few more moments before continuing. Up from the stairs came all the women of his household. His wife arrived, using a cane to walk up the stairs. His daughter also accompanied his wife, and she looked to be the same age as Rufus. She even looked a bit like him. They all came and greeted him with kisses and had a slave move one of the couches so that they could all see Caleb as he spoke.

"Woman, I told you!" he said. She bowed and spoke. "Yes, my lord, you were right," she said. Caleb had no idea what they were talking about.

"So, nephew, you are here for a reason, yes?" Cornelius asked.

"I am," he said. Caleb started to get nervous, as he was not sure where to start.

"Uncle, Auntie, I am a bit perplexed, and I thought you might be able to help me," he said. He fidgeted with his hands for a moment. His aunt spoke next.

"What is her name?"

"Yael," he said, looking down at the rooftop. He was ridiculously embarrassed that they could tell his words were already being tempered by the woman on his mind.

"She and I have committed to erusin, and I do not know of anyone else to talk to about my circumstance," he said. Finally, he looked up and each of them while he held his hands and continued.

"I was trained by your son, you know. He taught me to hunt, use weapons, control my thoughts and actions and dominate other men into submission. I do not know what I am to do with my skill. My future wife wants to be safe, and my life is about preparing for danger. I do not know how to reconcile these life demands. Since you were a soldier and are also a follower of Yeshua, I hoped that you would be able to guide me," he said.

"Give it to him, old man!" said Cornelius's wife. Caleb did not know what she was talking about, so he quickly stood up and handed Cornelius his son's ring.

"Boy, keep that! That isn't what she is talking about. Hold on, I will be right back," he said. It took the old man a few moments to get up and go downstairs. While he was gone, the two women asked Caleb many questions about Yael. As Cornelius returned, his daughter looked at him and shared.

"We look forward to meeting her soon."

The comment seemed odd to him. There were no plans for Yael to come here. Perhaps she meant at their wedding, but he did not see them traveling from here all the way to their wedding. Finally, Cornelius returned. Caleb politely nodded to the women before Cornelius handed him a large, rolled parchment. It looked identical to the one Eliza carried, but this one was thicker.

"This came last week on the same boat that carried the emperor's death announcement. I think some of your questions about what is next in your life are in there," said Cornelius. Caleb unwound the scroll and read it while Cornelius got all of their teacups refilled.

Honorable Cornelius of Caesarea,

Greetings to you and your house from all at the House of Flavian. It has been more than ten years since we have seen each other. I wished that I could be with you instead of sending you this message.

As you may have heard, your son and my friend Rufus died. That man fell in love with the people of Judah after we defeated their resistance in Jerusalem, and he remained with his new friend Mishi after his retirement. I am sorry I was not able to join your entire family at their wedding, but I am glad that you were able to make it to that small village and be there for those young people.

Just yesterday, Rufus's adopted nephew showed me his battle skills. The young man performed well in the Colosseum. I think you would have been proud, and the results showed this. I could see that Rufus had trained him, and this young man controlled his emotions and fought with his mind as much as his weapons.

He came to me with a young Hebrew girl. I could have killed her for speaking to me, but something that Rufus called the Holy Spirit came upon me, and I was instead willing to hear her speak. For her part, this girl was most courageous, perhaps even more so than many of my best leaders. She spoke as if she was following an untrodden path into my soul. I know you have tried to reach me in that regard, but she was successful.

I tell you this, my friend, she helped me see that I am a sinner. Yes, you and your son also told me this, but your words took fourteen years to take roots. Now, you are an old man and only get to see the fruit of the tree you planted when your days are few. Thank you for your commitment all these years.

When the young man left, I offered him a job training my elite soldiers. The empire cannot be built without the discipline that this young man demonstrated. He has proven to be a sharp killer, yet he needs instruction. The morning after his day in the glory of the Colosseum, he came to breakfast, and he was exhausted, even though his fight was over before water could boil. He needs help to understand his role as a judge and a leader. He does not know how to process what is expected of him. Perhaps you could finish the training that your son started?

He goes by Caleb of Tamar. Based on the conversation that I heard him speaking to his two sisters, I think he will be visiting you.

Lastly, there is the matter of this girl teacher. She is unique, and I feel endeared to her. I gave her a ring of our house, and you know what power that affords her. She is meant to teach. Alas, she also needs a teacher! She needs no confidence, but she will need some encouragement and some examples to follow to sharpen her craft. She has an exceptionally soft spot for family, and she needs someone like your wife to help prepare her for life in that God-awful place.

I think the message that she is to offer the men of our military is greater in worth than the extra coin we give to centurions like you for women of the night and drinking. Do you not agree?

After she left me and began her travels home, I was encouraged by the local teachers here to ask Yeshua to show me His plan for this girl. I tell you as I write this that I am using words I have never used. Her words were more powerful than anyone who has ever spoken to me in this palace. With the ring she wears, she is immune to the penalty of death for what my Senate tells me is blasphemy. I can exempt her from any crime, but the Senate will oppose me and present reasons why I am incorrect in my assessment of what is best for the empire. Perhaps this boy Caleb can be her protector. He already wears a ring that confers great power to him. I am considering making the rank on his ring effective, installing him as a centurion first, responsible for the men who oversee the protection of the royal household. The Senate will approve this. Can you arrange for him to complete his training and provide him with the soldiers he needs to protect her as she shares the greatest story ever told to my men?

As I finish this request and ponder my own words, there is one thing that this young Hebrew girl did that impacted me the most. She took all the coin that Caleb earned for his efforts in my Colosseum and gave it to me in exchange for a slave's freedom. This was the most unique act I have seen since I became the emperor. Whatever lived in her heart that made her want to do that, I yearn for it. Perhaps one day, I will have what this young one already has. Based on the heart of that boy, I think he has not yet discovered that he has feelings for that slave girl. For what it is worth, my concubine was very excited to see her freed to go home.

 Blessings to your wife and daughter. Take care of these young people that will be coming your way. Although they will not be the leaders of our empire, they will be the next generation of leaders of our faith. They are seekers, this generation. They want the truth. Then, when they find it, they tell you about it, even if you do not ask!

 Thank you, my uncle, for the investment you have made for all of us. I am a better man today because of you. May Yeshua become the true leader of this empire.

Sincerely,
Titus Flavian, Emperor

 Caleb looked up, speechless, but only for a moment.

 "So, the emperor knew I would come to you? How is that possible?" he said, shaking his head in disbelief.

"That is irrelevant. Young man, take that letter home and read it out loud. Give those girls a hug and let them all know that they are welcome here," he said.

"Uncle, Auntie, cousin, I would like for you to come to our wedding and meet them. I think it wise that they get to know you first. Isn't that wise?" Caleb said.

"He sounds like our son!" said his wife. They all laughed.

"Enough of this, let's get some food in you. We are being rude. After we eat, I will need to hear some recent stories," Cornelius said. Both his wife and daughter nodded in agreement. They ate their meal together, and Caleb sped through the timeline of events since he got the ring from Rufus until he left Tamar to come here. No one interrupted him, and it was dark outside before he was finished.

Cornelius left the women to continue making a new mat from some recently harvested grasses, and Cornelius took Caleb outside to sit under the stars and look at the heavens.

"When there is no moon, looking at the stars in the winter and spring gives the mind great clarity, so I have found," Cornelius said. They walked to the edge of the walled compounds, stepped through the wrought iron gate, and looked down at sea with the stars hovering over the horizon. Caleb finally felt the confidence to talk.

"Uncle, my future wife told me that she must feel safe. This is not negotiable for her. I, like you and your son, am a trained fighter, and I often find myself in harm's way. Perhaps the one word that least applies to who I am is 'safe.' How do we reconcile these things and become a family?"

Cornelius smiled and let a single exhale come from his mouth as he nodded his head.

"When my parents arranged for our marriage, I did not know that this thing was also important to my erusin. When

I saw her, I only saw her beauty and her smile. I thought, 'Surely, she is all I need to be complete.'"

He leaned back and laughed after hitting Caleb on the thigh.

"You decided to get to know your bride first. That, my boy, is the sharpest two edge sword in the empire! The way you described her inside made it seem like she was your rock and your affirmation. Now, she is a liability to you, and it makes no sense what the next step might be."

He allowed Caleb a moment to nod in agreement. No matter how terse this man might be, he was intuitive and saw through the outside shell quickly.

"As the local judge in this village, it was my job to keep order and to keep peace. Since I was the top man, that meant I had to kill when a man crossed a line that he knew not to cross, even after receiving grace. They are miserable moments. When my wife would see me come home with the blood of men on my face and hands, she would look at me like I was from Hades. You know what I told her?"

He knew to wait for Caleb to process his words before proceeding with the answer.

"All peace requires there first to be conflict. I will handle the conflict. You handle keeping the peace."

Caleb ruminated on those words while Cornelius continued.

"Who does your erusin have for counsel?" he asked.

"Eliza is probably her biggest one," he said.

"Oh, she won't work. She teaches the words of Yeshua. She is not safe. Who else?" the old man asked.

"I guess my aunt, but—" Cornelius cut him off.

"Boy, here is my plan for you then. Why do not you get married and come live with us? I will complete your training, and my wife can teach your wife to be a woman of Yahweh.

Solomon thought this was a good idea. Consider yourself both to be in training for a season," he said.

The two men looked forward as they watched a shooting star cross above the water's surface then disappear.

"Or two," said Cornelius, leaning over and touching his head on Caleb's shoulder.

"Uncle?" Caleb asked.

"Or two seasons. Come stay with us for a few seasons, and we will help you finish your education," he said.

Caleb had clarity. This place was working. This place would be his home, and he could see himself replacing Cornelius one day. Caleb had the peace he was looking for.

"Okay, we will do it," he said.

"Good work to make that decision, nephew! Now, tomorrow will be a bit long and long-winded for you because I am going to take you down to the wharf and introduce you to our leadership since you will be working with them for a few seasons. Then the day after tomorrow, we will put you on your horse and send you off to complete your erusin!"

Caleb smiled. "Uncle, I like those two ideas a lot!" he said.

"Here, take this note and put it with your belongings," Cornelius said as he offered Caleb the scroll from Titus.

"Does it matter that he is no longer the emperor?" he asked.

"Of course, it does. But his ideas were still good ones, don't you think?"

Caleb continued to stare straight ahead as a shower of meteors crossed the horizon in front of them.

"Well, then, there is your sign, boy. Now, it is now off to bed."

As they walked back, Cornelius took his arm for support.

"Caleb, my boy, there will never be safety in this world."

"Uncle, I killed men on three different occasions before my bar mitzvah. Trust me. I understand what you just said."

"My point is that you and I will always have a different and unique understanding of what the word 'safe' means compared to our women. That is perfectly okay. I will help you make peace with this. And my wife will teach your wife," Cornelius finished and patted Caleb's arm as he led them back into the house.

BEFORE THE WEDDING

The girls were already in Correae by the time Caleb arrived with Cornelius and his family's entourage. Caleb galloped ahead when they were close, so he could see the girls alone for a few moments. He bypassed village protocol and tied off the horse at his aunt and uncle's house, running directly into the kitchen. Katya was cooking dinner, and Matthew was mixing a brew of herbs and broth that all pregnant women take to ensure their future child's well-being.

"Where are Eliza and Yael?" he said, not waiting to catch his breath.

"Hello, my nephew," said his proud aunt. "Come give me a kiss," she mandated. He complied, and she offered him some food.

"No, thank you, Uncle Cornelius has more good food with him on his cart for a two-day journey than we had out on the ship for two weeks!" he said.

"There will be many guests arriving in these next few days, and I will need to keep a pot of hot water on the stove at all times. Can you help us out and get some more wood and bring it in the kitchen?"

With that last sentence, Katya broke eye contact and left the house, but she kept talking, albeit a bit louder since she was walking away.

"Don't stack it up higher than I can reach, Caleb, especially since I am pregnant. Also, get some fat from the village pits. I hate starting a fire the old way this time of the year," she added. She said the last words, nearly screaming, as she entered her mother's house to talk to her about something else.

"I guess I know where my mom got that from," he said under his breath.

Caleb decided he was hungry, after all. Maybe he was bored since none of the girls were here, and that was why he galloped here in the first place.

Yael and Eliza walked into the kitchen next. Eliza ran to her father and kissed him three times, as did Yael. All Caleb could do was stare at Yael and smile. Matthew figured out what was on his mind, and all he could do was smile back. Caleb reminded him of his own wedding ceremony to Katya some fifteen years earlier.

"Kids, come sit with your father for a moment before your mother gets back and some of our honored guests arrive."

They all came into the kitchen and sat cross-legged next to Matthew.

"When I married your mother, I had just spent several months building this home. My hands were raw from all the work, and, Eliza, your grandfather was at least as tired as I was. Back then, we did not get help from slaves with our homes. Do you know why I worked that hard? I did not want to wait one more day than required to become my Katya's husband. Since you are all old enough and family, I will now tell you that I greatly desired her to the point that there was nothing else on my mind. One time, I hit my hand with a hammer, and in that moment, I did not care because I knew that we would finish our home the very next day, and we could then finalize our wedding date. It was worth it. You two have taken a most unique route, and Caleb, you have a house already built that you own. You have offers to build on donated land near Gaza. I am one of many who want to know, what are you going to do?"

"That is why I arrived here ahead of Cornelius and his family. Yael, we really have to talk. Eliza, this concerns you as much as us, so please stay. I will be right back," he said.

He ran to his horse and retrieved the letter from Titus and gave it to Eliza to read out loud. As she was unrolling it, Katya walked back in with her mother. Matthew raised his hand, signaling her not to talk.

Eliza skimmed the note before she started reading.

"This is from the emperor, and it was addressed to Cornelius."

She paused and shook her head.

"Sister, you and I are both in here!" she said.

"Read it! Read it!" her mother yelled at her to start verbalizing the contents.

As she read it, Caleb wanted to hold Yael's hand again and let her hear everything as one flesh with him. However, he knew that he must wait another three days. He wished that they were getting married this afternoon.

As Eliza got to the end and read the signature out loud for all to hear, no one said anything. Caleb expected that. After all, it is not every day the emperor speaks about you to someone else.

"First of all, when Cornelius gave me that letter, he told me to go back and hug all the women in my life. I honor that request now."

He hugged Eliza first, then Katya and her mother. Finally, he turned to embrace Yael and stopped. She turned to her head to the side, awaiting him to take her in his arms.

He stood but only for a moment before his uncle's words resurfaced.

"You are a leader, and leaders prove themselves in difficult situations by exercising restraint. Kill when you must. Cross boundaries, but only if you have no choice."

"Yael, I love you and am in love with you. However, we made a promise to be pure before we married. Not that a hug between us with our family all around is the same as a broken promise. I promise to take you in my arms with unconditional love in three days. Okay?" he knew he needed to ask. She needed to willingly agree to this as his partner in life.

"Yes, I can wait. And, Caleb, what you just did makes me feel safe," she said. With that event now in the past, he started a conversation about the letter.

"I have been pondering this for the last few days, and I have talked to Uncle Cornelius about this. He understands me, Yael. I need his training if I am going to live a life with you that allows you to feel safe. I want to marry and immediately travel to Caesarea for a few seasons, so we can both be mentored."

Yael nodded as soon as he finished asking. Caleb's smile upon seeing her agreement turned into jumping up and down long enough to get everyone to laugh. Everyone added their opinion about what else he should do, but for now, he had the encouragement he needed to retain hope.

Late that day, Zev arrived with Dor and Benji and two volunteers from Gaza. They all greeted everyone, and Zev was immediately taken to Katya's mother and father's home for a celebratory meal and a small inclusion ceremony that formally brought Zev into the house in Correae. Matthew watched the entire event, but he left early. Later in the evening, while it was still light enough to walk around, Matthew took Yael, Caleb, and Zev on a brief tour of their mining operations, reminding them of the responsibility associated with the knowledge of this place's existence. He told them with no uncertainty that all who know the secret of this mine must let that secret die with them if they are captured.

"Is this the secret that Eliza was talking about at our ceremony in Kedron that grieved her?" Yael asked.

"It must be," said Caleb. When they were done and walked back into the house, Matthew announced to everyone that he had just given them a tour of the mine. Everyone was sitting on the floor, but they all stopped talking to make eye contact with those who just learned their secret.

"For Yael and myself, your secret is safe with us," said Caleb.

"I, as well," said Zev.

The family rearranged their places on the floor, allowing a space for everyone to sit. And with that act, all the secrets that had separated them were exposed. They were finally family by all measures.

WEDDING DAY

The following morning, the last of the guests arrived. The village started their weddings in the winter and spring later in the day to allow for late guests and cooler weather. This day appeared to be the first warm day of the spring season, and no one would need warm cloaks for the ceremony.

The older men in the village slaughtered, prepared, and did all the work in the cooking pits. They also did all the sauce preparation and bread making, and sometimes women would come over and see how well they were doing, often making unsolicited suggestions that were not well-received. However, what their choice to do all the food prep provided was a chance for the women to enjoy all the buildup to the wedding that the men typically did not care about. The women made a fuss over the appearance of all the people in the wedding party, and no one held back, pulling out all the gold jewelry and artifacts from the village vaults for everyone to see.

Eliza, Yael, and Katya each wore pure white clothing, with Yael choosing to wear what she wore during her worship dance. Caleb got groomed completely and put on the battle attire of a centurion, including getting a brand-new scabbard for his ceremonial sword. Neither Yael nor Eliza were willing to remove their necklaces, but Eliza was given a crown that matched Yael's, but hers was made of gold. They wore golden bangles on each arm, and silver jeweled chains donned their ankles.

Benji was to oversee the reading of the *Sheva B'rachot*, or seven blessings. He would also walk ahead of the bride, groom, and their families down to the water's edge. He also carried the glass that Caleb would step on and break before all the guests would shout, "*Mazel tov!*"[11]

For Caleb, all thoughts associated with his desire to be with Yael were lost this day, as it was required that he fast from the previous night until their ceremony was complete.

The village elders who were not cooking all wore sackcloth and did all the menial labor associated with the celebration, setting an example of servant leadership for all the youth to see. They set up the altar, the *chuppah*, and all the benches where the family would sit.

After the sun had crossed mid-day, the ceremony commenced. Zev, Matthew, and all the men either sat or stood on the right side of the chuppah. Eliza, Katya, and all the women were on the left. As they went down the aisle, Benji spoke loud enough for all to hear.

"Caleb, you may hold your bride's hand," and with those words, Caleb reached over and took her hand, forgetting about any sense of hunger. Once they reached the altar, Caleb and Yael each signed their ketubah, and it was signed by Benji and Dor as non-family witnesses. Caleb then reached under his tunic and took out Yael's *bedeken*, or veil, and he covered her face for the remainder of the ceremony. Eliza stepped behind the altar with Dor and read the seven blessings out loud for all to hear. She was most impressive in her memorization of Hebrew words, seldom used in speech anymore.

Once they finished, Caleb held both of Yael's hands as Dor placed the wedding glass on the ground in front of them, and they each said a blessing. Then, Caleb crushed the glass, and everyone yelled out, "Mazel tov!" and the wedding crowd applauded and clapped. Caleb kissed Yael for the first time and turned her toward the audience for all to see her. Her veil removed, he spoke out loud with great pride.

"My wife. Bless her, indeed!" and everyone chimed in with equal blessings for her.

The two of them went into the *yichud* room. It is here that the bride and groom get their first intimate time. They also ate some food to break their fast. When they emerged, nearly everyone was there, congratulating them with hugs and handshakes. They walked to the village center, where a large table was placed. On it were many gifts from everyone who was invited. The mayor stepped up and spoke on behalf of the village.

"Caleb and Yael, you are now husband and wife. Congratulations to you both! To begin, the table that holds all of your gifts was made by my father. It is your gift. He asks that you put it in your kitchen!"

For the next window of time, as the final steps of the meal preparation were made, each family took the center of the square and gave the newlyweds a gift. Katya's parents gave them a parcel of land next to Matthew and Katya. Zev reiterated his commitment to come and help build their home once they settle on a place.

The men from Gaza gave them a scroll telling Caleb to read it out loud.

Two first-class roundtrip tickets to Massilia, with food and accommodations.

Both Caleb and Yael asked them where Massilia was.

"My friends, that is the port entryway into Gaul. Do not fret, young Yael, you need not stop in Rome to get there. It sails from either Caesarea or Joppa, once every two weeks," a man said. The two newlyweds looked at each other and smiled. Caleb was done holding back the affection he felt for Yael, as he was no longer was required to do so. Instead, he kissed her in front of everyone. More cheers erupted, so he did it again.

Once the applause and cheering neared an end, the village gave them three purses of coin, and with each came an explanation from the elders who spoke to Eliza before she left to travel to Correae.

"This first bag of coin goes to all newlyweds, so you have no concern with income the first six months you are married. The second bag comes from what is due to you as a reward for rescuing your parents from slavery. The third bag comes with the expectations that you give it to fellow Hebrews who need help."

Both Caleb and Yael bowed and thanked them.

As they neared the end, the mayor came back up and asked Caleb and Yael to come forward, and he asked them to say what was next in their lives. They held hands, and Caleb spoke first.

"My wife and I both seek to know the truth. We want to expand what we think are our horizons, as we have already tasted what this looks like. It is both full of wonder and beauty, and it is also full of danger that can cause a lifetime of damage. For now, I made a promise to the man whom I fought side by side with, and my uncle taught me to honor my promises," he paused long enough to find Cornelius in the crowd and nodded at the man. Cornelius, for his part, put his arm around his wife and pulled her into him as tears flowed from her eyes. It was in the life of Caleb that her son continued to influence the world.

"My wife and I will be moving to Caesarea for a season or two to train with my great uncle. I have accepted a position as protectorate over the royal family," he shared. Everyone applauded, for they all had seen Eliza's ring and knew that he would be continuing his epic journey of taking care of the one who wears it. Since Domitian was the emperor, its power remained.

While everyone applauded the announcement, Cornelius slowly made his way to the table at the center of the village. He handed Caleb another scroll.

"Read it out loud, boy!" he said.

By Senatorial Decree

We appoint Caleb of Correae as a centurion in charge of protecting any royal entourage that travels within the borders of the great Roman Empire.

Signed
Domitian Flavian

Before anyone could say anything, Cornelius took his helmet and gave it to Caleb.

"This is what a centurion wears when he is at work. It reminds him of who he serves during his waking hours. Each time I put it on, I am reminded that the Messiah was a carpenter, not far from here, in fact. When He went to work, He took tools, but He did not let those tools become His identity. His identity remained in the Father, and the Father remained in Him. I had a reminder put inside of it, and I look at it each time I put it on. Read it out loud, but look at that girl of yours when you do it."

Caleb was stunned. The first man of any significance he ever killed was a centurion. His work that day haunted him and kept him awake at night until he could not live with himself. Now, he was that man, and he could see the circle of life coming back around. He could see that he could easily become as evil and powerfully rich as the man he killed and that one day, others like him will come to replace him and take him down if he does not exercise self-control. He wanted to cry, but he felt it shameful now that he was a centurion in the Roman military, a position considered the most honorable and trustworthy within the empire. Instead, he paused a few moments before speaking. Eliza could see what was happening, and she approached her cousin and spoke quietly, so only Cornelius and Yael could also hear her.

"Caleb, do not fear. Right now, I am still with you," she said. With that, Caleb took a deep breath in and exhaled, allowing a single tear to fall.

"That is okay, boy. I learned to cry a long time ago. Just do not do it when the enemy is watching, okay?" Cornelius said, causing another round of laughter.

"It is from King David," said Cornelius. Caleb turned the helmet upside down and read it out loud for the first time.

"Remember who you serve when you put this on: first, Yeshua, second, Yael."

No one spoke for a few moments.

"I had them add your wife's name to that since she will be the one who travels through life by your side, just like this helmet will. David did not talk about your wife, did he? Remember, it isn't the military you serve. They can be some real ruthless bastards sometimes. Make a go of it, boy. I wore that thing during my ministry. I think you can do the same. I will teach you how," he said, pulling in Caleb for a big hug. Caleb gave up his protection and allowed himself to cry deep and long tears. Eliza hugged Yael as those two always did when someone cried or was in trouble.

Cornelius had already started his mentorship of Caleb, and he began in the place where it should be second nature. It is the places where we live that we need to sensibly integrate faith and work. Cornelius saw that the best place to start was with inscriptions inside of the helmet as he got dressed for work each day. Yael decided she liked how Cornelius was mentoring her husband.

As the evening festivities were coming to an end, people went off to find lodging for the night. Caleb and Yael would stay in Eliza's grandparents' home, as they had an unused room. Eliza and Zev would stay at Katya and Matthew's house. Cornelius brought a large tent, and he would camp on the plot of land that Caleb just inherited.

DEPARTURES FROM THE PAST

The following morning, all the remnants of the wedding converged on Katya's kitchen for breakfast. Although the room was small, a dozen people occupied that space. Katya gave the slaves the morning off, and the two women from Cornelius's family took over much of the cooking and food preparation. They all realized that the last time they were in this kitchen together was when Yael and Mishi came back from Jerusalem fifteen years ago.

Matthew talked to Cornelius at length about the Roman efforts around the walls of Jerusalem, and he shared that Roman efforts were to make a part of the city a refuge for gentiles of wealth. Efforts were underway to remove the Hebrew artifacts from the Temple Mount, but only a few monuments remained standing, including a large wall. Matthew speculated that the city would soon be void of its religious significance, and he thought he had heard a conversation of a new temple dedicated to Jupiter Capitolinus that was in the design stage. Cornelius shook his head in disgust.

"Roman bastards! I wish that I weren't one of them!" he said.

Throughout the morning, the smell of the cooking fire was strong, but the quality of the conversation was even stronger, as they all got to connect with each other in deep conversation. Finally, as the meal was nearing completion, Katya took command of the conversation as was proper for a woman in a Hebrew kitchen.

"I gave the slaves the day off so all of us could have some family time. Weddings are meant to bring us together, but we live distant lives and are too busy to keep up with each other. With our newlyweds leaving for their new lives later today, I thought we should come together and extend to them blessings for the life they will navigate together."

Matthew nodded and agreed with his wife. However, Matthew's intention was to take the conversation in a new direction that was long overdue.

"I also wish to add that none of us have shared how our hearts were broken when our Yael and Mishi were killed, as was Rufus. All of us grieved in our own way, but we did it apart from each other. This is not our way, and we know that these are trying times that test our hearts. I would like us all to share a story of each of them and their impact on us. They were the original seekers from our union. Without them and the risks that they took, none of us would be here."

No one could respond to the emptiness that came from this request for a funeration other than to agree that it was overdue in their hearts.

"I will start," said Katya. She finished drying her hands while Yael took some of her loose hair and pulled it from her face. The two of them smiled as she came to their circle and sat down. Her two daughters remained standing as she spoke.

"If you told me that my little sister would become my daughter's hero, I would think you to be crazy. If you told me that she would change the hearts of hundreds of thousands, I would think you crazy. If you told me she would get killed by a Roman blade defending her husband, now, that I would believe! She would fight for what she believed in, and I do not think she would feel ashamed of the way she lived or the way she died. Just this morning, as I was speaking to my daughters, I could see that she will be with me when we all gather for the high holidays. My one daughter was her student. My other daughter bears her name. If the child in my womb is a girl, I shall name her Yael, after my sister."

With that, her girls sat down next to her, and both embraced her in a heartfelt hug. Cornelius's wife put her head on her husband's shoulder and let some tears fall.

Dor spoke next.

"I remember listening to Mishi at a gathering when I was a young boy less than Caleb's age. I thought I was going to join the military and fight against the Romans alongside the Maccabees. It turns out that I joined the fight, but I chose the side of our Messiah! It was Yael, though, who shared messages that impacted me the most. As some of you already know, I have called Eliza to follow me. It would be a lie to say that her aunt's teaching skills did not impact my choice. I am honored to get a chance to share with young Eliza what her aunt shared with me."

Eliza tried to smile in gratitude, but only tears would come. Yael held her, rubbing and kissing her head just like the two of them did on the boat ride home from Rome. The wounds from losing her hero had not healed, but these words were part of that path or recovery from loss. No one in the room knew this more than Dor.

Rufus's mother spoke next.

"Our son would write home to us, and literally every letter contained stories of what he saw happening as he traveled to different synagogues around the empire to share. He felt so honored to be a part of Mishi and Yael's ministry. And, in every letter, he reminded us to pray for Titus and his family.

I tell you the truth: he said that in every letter. Sometimes, I would read his letters to our synagogue in Caesarea, and Hebrew and gentile alike would come together and hold hands, lifting that man to heaven for redemption."

She paused to wipe tears from her eyes before she continued, "Even after hearing everyone's story, we are still in awe at how Yahweh answered all of the prayers we said over this man for years. I tell you the truth, I was discouraged. It is only now that I see that Yahweh's timeline is not the same as ours. Young Eliza, Yahweh picked you to disciple long before Dor did." Everyone nodded their heads, and Katya allowed Eliza to place her head on her shoulder, imitating what Cornelius's wife did with him.

Caleb and Eliza chose to go last.

Caleb looked up at Cornelius and spoke for all to hear, but it was an intimate conversation meant for only him.

"Uncle, I am truly trusting the well-being of my family in you. At first, I was scared when I met you because I thought you were an old man wandering around without a mind. I had no idea you were evaluating me. When I learned that, I also felt some shame about not seeing what was in front of me. After listening to you now, it seems like the first steps on life's journeys are always full of fear, aren't they?" he asked that only rhetorically, but he kept speaking.

"I know these are only words, but thank you, in advance, for investing in my wife and me. If my parents were still here, they would say the same thing," he said.

"Go!" Cornelius's wife looked at her husband, commanding him publicly. This was all but blasphemy within their faith, but everyone could see that her heart was that of encouragement, not one of demand or disrespect. Cornelius nodded his head in agreement and stood up. He retrieved a chair and placed it in front of Caleb. He sat down in it, and his wife came with him. She placed her hands on his shoulders. Everyone could see Cornelius's face as he spoke. He closed his eyes as he began.

"I lost my only son just a few months ago. My wife and I were lamenting that we never got to give him the blessings rightly due to him as my firstborn. This old woman behind me gave me the idea that perhaps I should give them to you. So, Caleb, I call you as my adopted son: come sit in front of me and receive your father's birthright."

All the men stood and walked to Cornelius, reaching out and placing a hand on his. However, it was also now time for his wife to begin her mentorship.

"Yael, little one, come kneel behind your husband and hold his shoulders. Bow your head and pray for him as my husband extends all that he has into your man. Anytime you see Caleb misbehaving in the future, and I promise you he will misbehave, remember this moment, and pray for the spirit that you are about to see return and cover this man. This is the Holy Spirit, in His glory, doing a job that only He can do. You cannot do this act, Little One. He is not your man. He belongs to Yeshua."

"Yes, mom," she said, not hesitating to extend the highest possible regard a Hebrew woman can offer to another. She did not hesitate and did what was asked of her. Eliza remained seated, unsure what to do.

"Girl, go sit with your sister! This is a bad time to leave her alone," said Cornelius's wife. Everyone chuckled as Eliza got up and quickly moved next to Yael, kissing her on the cheek. "I love you, my sister. I will pray with you," she said. Katya got up and joined her daughters, all of them kneeling behind Caleb.

"Yahweh from ancient times past, You gave this tradition to the family of Abraham, to Isaac, and to Jacob. Per their great example, I ask that all the blessings that a father can bestow be given to his young man. Fill him with all the blessings that I should have passed to Rufus, and I pray that he passes forward these blessings to his sons in the future."

"And daughters."

Cornelius looked up at Eliza.

"What?" he said.

"And daughters," she said, repeating herself. "Fathers should also bless their daughters like they bless their sons. Girls deserve it just as much as boys do," she said.

Cornelius was in a state of shock. He turned to look at his wife for guidance.

"Don't look at me," said his wife. "This girl is right, though, and you know it!" she added after he looked at Eliza.

"And daughters!" said Cornelius. "Little One, if you were not to become a rabbi, I would reprimand you. Perhaps because you are, I should reprimand you!" he said. That made everyone erupt in laughter. Cornelius then finished his prayer.

"Father, I pray that he passes forward these blessings both to his sons and daughters in his future."

Eliza ran to the old man and kissed him on the cheek. He pulled her in for an embrace and turned to Dor.

"Dor, I hope you know what you are getting into, choosing one like this to be your disciple!" gesturing for Dor to come to this elderly statesman as well for a kiss and a hug.

Finally, Eliza's turn to speak came up.

"Everything you say about me and Aunt Yael being my hero is true. She had power with words, and she had no fear of using them, even though they caused her death. Even now, I spoke boldly to a man who was blessing my cousin, and I ask forgiveness for disrespecting your authority, Uncle Cornelius."

She paused.

"Little One, we old people need some correction now and then," he lifted his hands as a sign for her to return to him. He kissed her three times as a father would kiss a daughter, and she reciprocated.

"However, as I was listening to you all of you, I realized two things. First, yes, I am willing to be a rabbi for my faith. Dor, I accept your offer and will come back to you once my mother has delivered her child and is able to care for the baby on her own. Second, and perhaps more importantly, if I am to serve Yahweh, I need to trust Him. When I heard the emperor's words and the role that Caleb is taking, I saw how Yahweh was using the moment to instruct us all."

She pulled Titus's ring from her finger.

"The emperor created a position for Caleb to protect members of the royal house. That will not work if my sister is not a member of royalty."

She walked over to Yael and put the ring on her middle finger, kissing her on the cheek.

"Will you please take this? Your husband will need you next to him to offer him the affection and affirmation that you and I both know that he needs. You can only be there with him on his assignments if you are also royalty."

The room was silent. Eliza openly relinquished the artifact that made her the most powerful Hebrew in all of Judah.

"Good idea," said Cornelius.

Eliza continued, "And if I am to trust the Creator with my well-being, I cannot also be trusting immunity that the emperor extended me with this ring. What kind of hypocritical teacher will that make me?" she said. Nearly everyone in the room nodded. Yael turned to her husband, and he nodded to her in acceptance of the gift. Yael rotated the ring and put it on her finger, showing the insignia of the House of Flavian.

"I do not know what to say!" Yael said.

"Oh, not this again!" said Eliza, looking to diffuse the moment. It worked, as everyone laughed. Yael blushed at her inability to receive gifts.

"Not even in the darkest of my days in Rome did I think that any of this love was possible. Thank you, sister."

With that, their impromptu funeral ended. Zev announced that he would be returning to finish work at the House of Healing but then would move to finish his life in Correae, and one of the families there thought that they might know of a good woman that he could marry. Everyone applauded this idea, and they offered him many congratulations.

Everyone stood and began their goodbyes. Cornelius and his entourage left first, and Yael rode next to Cornelius's wife while Caleb rode on a horse with Cornelius ahead of their cart. Dor and Benji left on a small cart with Zev. Before midday, all the out-of-town guests would leave the valley that Correae was in, and they would take separate paths to reach their destination. The rabbis would go south towards Kedron while Cornelius's group would head west towards Caesarea.

Once the dust of their departure was settled, Eliza returned to her parents' home. She went into the kitchen where her mom was cleaning, and she put her head on her shoulder.

"I hope this is not a pattern. You left home alone, and look at what happened to you!" her mother said.

"What?" said Eliza, returning to her role as the teenage daughter of a simple woman.

"You are an adventure seeker, like your sister who just left! You each left us and went out alone, looking for the

Of Healing and Finding Home

truth. You each came home with newer and better relationships. You scared us all, Little One," she said. "And you are going to be a rabbi! I can still hardly form the words!" Katya said as she finished sweeping the floor. "Come, Little One, let's go down to the river," she said, acting like the mother that she was.

The walk was short, and they went downstream away from the gold mining commotion and sat on some rocks that had been piled into seating years ago. Eliza put her head on her mother's shoulder.

"Mother, when you told me that you were jealous of Auntie, what did you mean?" she asked.

"Even since your auntie was young, she was willing to take risks and explore. She heard stories about others who failed, but it did not deter her. They did deter me. Although she is not here, she had a very rich life and impacted hundreds of thousands of people. I wish I had impacted hundreds of thousands," she said, letting a chuckle out.

"Mother, you impacted me more than anyone else in the world. Isn't that enough?"

"Of course it is!" she said, and they both hugged.

"Oh, Little One, you have already impacted more than that by your antics in the Colosseum and the palace, I think. Who knows how many others you impacted with your time in the House of Healing and on Calabria? You must take the time to see that the very thing the men from Gaza and your family in Caesarea prayed for came to pass with you. All this time, you were seeking Yahweh when He already picked you."

Eliza nodded her head as the impact of her mother's statement began to set in.

"Mom, what is a good number of children to have?" she asked.

"Well, now, aren't we planning?" her mom chided her. "How many do you want to have, Eliza?" she said.

"Mother, I do not know. I was just thinking that if men who are rabbis have family and children, then I should, too, right?"

"Here is what I know. If your husband disagrees with you, he will need to take it to Caleb and Yael first. I would not want to cross paths with a centurion or a member of the royal house who are both Yeshua followers. Oh, that would be a bad day for your husband."

They both laughed.

"Mother, I love you. I am glad you are here with me."

With that, Eliza finally had peace. Her future remained clouded, but so did her past only three months ago.

"Mother, you know every place that I went, I was uncomfortable. I was not comfortable on the boat to Rome. I hated Rome. I hated the palace. The boat ride home with Yael was anything but a homecoming. The only thing that felt comfortable was giving my sister that ring earlier today. Do you know that?" she shared.

"I do. As a little girl, you would always give your first and best findings to others," Katya said.

That comment reminded Eliza of the moment when she emptied her coin bag to Dor. That, too, was comfortable.

Eliza got up and stood at the edge of the river.

"Mother, I think I would like to be alone for a little while. I will be back later today. You need not worry about me, okay?" she said. She stood up and began walking towards the mountains that scared her mother and motivated her aunt. It was her turn to experience the Northerns, but this time with no fear that Yahweh could not help her overcome.

"I love you, Dear. Please be careful!" Katya said.

After a long morning of walking, Eliza reached an overlook that gave her a first look at both the Jabbok River and the River Jordan. Just a few months ago, she pressed her aunt to describe the place where she lost her virginity, and Eliza knew she had arrived there. She smiled and sat down, allowing a few tears to fall as the completeness of her journey reached fruition. Spring was on its way, and she could hear the sounds of the snowmelt and the rush of the water in the distance. She opened her mouth and spoke a sincere prayer.

"Yahweh, my aunt made a mistake in this place, and You used it for great good. I have traveled the world, and soon, I will be a rabbi, like my auntie before me."

She paused to allow deep, sobbing tears to flow from her eyes. She raised her hands, placing her knees on the ground, lifting her hands to heaven.

"I commit this place and this mountain range to being special for us. I will come here and pray to You while I await my mother's baby. Thank You, Yahweh, for honoring Your promises and showing me that You can use all things for good. Thank You for my desire to seek. It has brought me back home to You."

EPILOGUE

Although we have seen the end of two different Yaels, Eliza, Katya, and Caleb, these characters and their offspring will appear in future works. For those of you who have connected with them, you justify why I write.

In the Seekers series, everyone I wrote about makes a great discovery, and no two characters make their discovery in the same place. For some, it is on the deck of a sinking ship. Others got a glimpse of their wretchedness while holding a weapon. Finally, some found their worth standing next to those and uplifting others who stood in the gap between life and death. After all, there is no such thing as a school of interpersonal insight nor a university of meaningful growth. Life presents these schools and their classroom when we are deemed ready, even when we are not seeking them. We all have a few of them in our lifetime, and those who make them happen become dear to us.

My scoutmaster was one such person. Another one was my quantum mechanics instructor. A third was a business associate who stole from me. Of course, none have made a greater impact than my wife, but eternity has a calling on our souls that we drowned out with busyness to the point that it has become the topic of my next book.

At the start of the Seeker series, I created a spreadsheet of those who have come into my life and made a difference, as I am a seeker. I also have a column called "current status," and for the three of them, I wrote "needs improvement." Originally, I wrote "lost" for them, but I chose a path of hope, thinking that one day, the stars might align, and we can see that we all are brothers and sisters of the same God who made all things. In the last, He does make all things new, but I would prefer not to set things right after I reach eternity. Let's fix them now.

Go out there and love somebody. There is a great chance that they are seeking something, and you might be a part of that, even if only for a limited time. You may not get to take the ride with them to Rome and back, but you might touch their soul in the synagogue of life along the way.

ENDNOTES

1. Bar and *bat mitzvah* are Jewish coming of age ceremonies for youth as they become adults. Boys go through Bar mitavah, whereas girls experience bat mitzvah.
2. *Mohel* is a Jew trained in the practice of circumcision.
3. 1 Corinthians 7:18-19, NIV.
4. *Yarmulke* is a cap, made of cloth and worn by Jewish men.
5. My paraphrase of Psalm 56:8.
6. My paraphrase of Psalm 51:10-13, NCV.
7. *Beth midrash* is a Jewish school located in a synagogue.
8. *B'nai mitzvah* is a plural form for bar and bat mitzvah.
9. Luke 15:11-32, NIV.
10. *Chuppah* is a canopy under which a Jewish couple stand during their wedding. It can also mean the second stage of a Jewish marriage ceremony.
11. *Mazel tov* is a phrase used to express congratulations.

CPSIA information can be obtained
at www.ICGtesting.com
Printed in the USA
LVHW110046191021
700772LV00004B/91

9 781637 693742